AF539588

LONG LIVE KING KOBE

Following the Murder of Tyler Nichols

photographs and interviews
Spencer Ostrander

introduction and accompanying texts
Paul Auster

foreword
Sherma Chambers

It was the worst day of my life.

On December 23, 2020, I received a phone call that something had happened to my son, Tyler. In a panic, I rushed over to Methodist Hospital. While I was still in the car, my son Shomari called to tell me that Tyler hadn't made it, that he had died in the ambulance on the way to the emergency room. All I remember saying is: "Don't tell me my son is gone, don't tell me my baby is gone." Once I reached the hospital, other family members were there, and we were all told to go to the chapel to wait for the doctor. I felt numb. Tyler's girlfriend, Ashley, was screaming. When the doctor came in, he told me that I couldn't hold my baby because an investigation was underway and Tyler's body was evidence.

I went home. When we drove past the spot where Tyler had been attacked, the corner was roped off with yellow tape. Several policemen were there. I understood that this was a crime scene and that my baby had been murdered.

When I finally got to the house, it was crowded with friends and family, all of us in shock, all of us hugging each other and trying to understand what the hell had just happened. It was still almost unimaginable to accept that Tyler had been taken from us.

As I was planning Tyler's funeral, it became clear to me that my job going forward would be to carry on his name and legacy. Ashley was the one who came up with the name of the foundation we created: Long Live King Kobe. Its purpose is to reach out into the community and make contact with the boys in the street to show them that their lives can be different, better, to show them love. We will be talking to them at their schools and in their homes. Our goal is to open a community center where we can offer a safe haven for families and individuals who have suffered acts of violence and help them to heal through one-on-one and group sessions.

LLKK wants to help the boys of the street. Not only with love, but by teaching them that acts of violence devastate families and communities for generations, just as the four generations of my family have been devastated by Tyler's death.

At the funeral on January 10, 2021, a young man came up to me and introduced himself as Spencer Ostrander. He said that he was a photographer who had been working on a long-term project about gun violence in America and asked if I would give him permission to stay at the funeral and take pictures from the back of the room. We looked into each other's eyes, and then Spencer asked if he could give me a hug. I said yes. It was the most comforting hug I have ever received from a stranger.

The following week, as I was going through my pocketbook, I found the slip of paper that Spencer had used to write down his contact information and felt a sudden, powerful need to reach out to him. We arranged for him to come visit me at my house, and for two or three hours we sat in the living room and talked about Tyler and the family. I was not talking to a stranger anymore but to someone I had known for a long time—someone who had been sent to me for a reason.

Over the next weeks and months, Spencer returned to the house several times and got to know everyone in the family as well as Tyler's closest friends. He took photographs of all of us and sat down with each person individually for long talks about what we had been going through since Tyler's death. I am convinced that talking about our grief helped us.

The book you are holding in your hands was a group effort, a collaboration between our family and Spencer and his collaborator, Paul Auster. When Spencer came to the house in May and presented us with the first draft, I understood that this was the reason why he had been sent to me. My son Shayne, who was attacked with Tyler on the night his brother was killed, sat down and slowly went through the book, and when he was finished he lifted it up in his right hand and said: "This is the last five months of my life."

This book will tell our story and keep Tyler's legacy alive for generations.

–Sherma Chambers

It was a weird and senseless crime, a sudden, unprovoked burst of violence on a tranquil street in a tranquil Brooklyn neighborhood on the eve of Christmas Eve, and two minutes after the attack began, twenty-one-year-old Tyler Kobe Nichols collapsed onto the sidewalk with three knife wounds in the front of his torso and one in the back. He died in the ambulance on the way to the hospital.

Tyler and his twenty-four-year-old brother, Shayne, had gone out for holiday haircuts at a local barbershop just a few blocks from where they lived. They started home at around a quarter to eight, the only pedestrians on the empty streets during this dark, pandemic winter, and at the corner of Coney Island Avenue and Turner Place, within eyeshot of their own house, they noticed a car parked at the curb with two young men in it, both of them strangers. Double-parked beside that car was another car with three more young men in it, all of them strangers as well. For reasons unknown, the five unknowns were staring at the Nichols brothers.

"I looked in the car," Shayne told the *Daily News*, "and then two kids came out. They asked us what we were looking at. Then they just started fighting us." Seconds later, the three from the other car joined in the attack, and suddenly it was five against two. The brothers did what they could to defend themselves, but they were outnumbered and took their fair share of knocks. Unexpectedly, the three from the double-parked car suddenly stopped fighting, returned to their car, and drove off. A few moments after that, the first two piled into their car and drove off in the same direction. Shayne looked over at Tyler and said, "Let's go," but Tyler was unresponsive. "I think I got stabbed," he said, and then, according to Shayne, "he just dropped to the ground."

A twenty-one-year old kid goes out for a haircut and winds up bleeding to death on a Brooklyn sidewalk. "Nothing ever happens in this neighborhood," his brother told the *News*. "It's my first fight in the whole twenty years I've lived here."

Nor was robbery a motive in the attack, since the three hundred dollars in Shayne's wallet were untouched, as was the gold chain he was wearing around his neck. Had the stabbing been prompted by a gang initiation ritual—kill someone, anyone, in order to gain acceptance into the group—or was it simply a random act of brutality committed by an angry, nihilistic teenage boy? Impossible to say. And also impossible to say just now whether the suspect the police have tentatively identified as the killer will turn out to have been guilty of the crime.

I missed the story in the *News* and never would have learned of Tyler Nichols's death if not for the photographer Spencer Ostrander, who told me about it shortly after he made contact with the Nichols family. Roughly six months ago, I joined Ostrander in a project he had launched two years earlier on the epidemic of mass shootings that has spread across America in the past two decades. In that time, he has traveled widely through all regions of the country, taking photographs of more than two dozen sites where these killings have occurred—not from some sensationalist impulse to cash in on the horrors of American violence but from a personal commitment to memorialize those places as tokens of our collective national grief and force us to remember the savagery we have visited upon one another as bullet after bullet has wiped out thousands of innocent lives.

I have been enlisted to write the preface to this work-in-progress, and in the course of our discussions over the past months, Ostrander's project has expanded beyond the sinister phenomenon of mass shootings to take on the bigger question of American gun violence in general, which kills forty thousand and wounds eighty thousand men, women, and children every year. To that end, he has reached out to the survivors of gunshot wounds who are now permanently confined to wheelchairs, to the families of those who have been killed or wounded, and, with the permission of the parents, spouses, and relatives of the dead, has begun attending funerals of the victims.

In this instance, the director of the funeral home made a mistake and told Ostrander that Tyler Nichols had been killed by a gun. He suggested that Ostrander come to the funeral early, where he would introduce him to Tyler Nichols's mother, Sherma Chambers, who would decide whether to allow him to take pictures during the service, and so it was that the thirty-six-year-old Seattle-born photographer and the fifty-two-year-old working mother who was born on the island of Saint Vincent and has been living in Brooklyn for close to forty years met for the first time.

The encounter began with Ostrander looking straight into the eyes of the dead boy's mother, and a moment later his arms were around her, enveloping her in a great bear hug of solidarity and commiseration. As she later told him, she knew he was someone who could be trusted from the first instant they looked into each other's eyes. They had exchanged no more than a few words, but a human connection had been established between them, and Ostrander was granted permission to stay.

A week later, Sherma Chambers contacted her new ally and invited him to her house in Kensington for a fuller conversation about his project and to talk to him about her son. Ostrander was well aware by then that his presence there had nothing to do with his yearslong research into gun violence, but what did that matter? He had stumbled into the midst of a grieving household that was willing to share its stories with him and allow themselves to be photographed in their time of pain and mourning, and because Spencer Ostrander is a person of singular compassion and purity of purpose, the entire household was with him, understanding that they would not be exploited but instead would serve as exemplars of the binding human force that connects us in times of sorrow.

I look into your face and see myself. Such is the power of photographic portraiture when it manages to achieve its highest objective. *I become you.*

It is not possible to talk about Tyler Nichols's life without first understanding something about the house his family has owned since 1990, a three-story wooden structure with two front porches, a basement apartment, and a kitchen on every floor that has functioned historically as a small, self-contained village inhabited by members of the Nichols-Chambers family—a rock-solid, transgenerational household that has held fast in an age of ever-dwindling and ever more dispersed American families. On the day before Tyler's death, fifteen people were living there: Tyler, his two older brothers, Shayne and Shomari (29), his mother, his mother's mother and one of his mother's sisters, several of his first cousins, Shomari's wife, Vera, the couple's little daughter, Raine, Shayne's girlfriend, Brittany, and Tyler's girlfriend, Ashley, who had moved in three years earlier when she was eighteen (the two kids had met at school when they were eleven and had been in love ever since). Except for the little girl and her great-grandmother, everyone who lived in the house worked at a full-time job, everyone pitched in, everyone pulled together. None of that has changed since the night of December twenty-third. The only difference is that fourteen people live there now, not fifteen, and the space that Tyler occupied has been turned into an enormous hole.

It was that house, and that hole, that Ostrander walked into on the afternoon of his first visit, where one by one he talked to various members of the family about Tyler and asked them to sit for a preliminary round of photographs. For his second visit, he carried along a tape recorder and spent several hours conducting separate interviews with Tyler's mother, Sherma, his brothers Shayne and Shomari, Shomari's wife, Vera, and a twenty-eight-year-old first cousin, Kareem Eusebe, a college graduate with a degree in biomedical technology, and little by little a picture began to emerge of a last-born tyke tagging along after his older brothers until he was off to kindergarten and the grades beyond, at which point he began participating in after-school programs at P.S. 282 in Park Slope, where he studied and progressed at such divergent activities as fencing, the steel drums, and the piano, and then, as he moved into his late, preadolescent boyhood, his passion for skateboarding, for which he showed an immense talent, far surpassing the abilities of his older brother, Shayne, and as the clock ticked on and he entered middle school in Ditmas Park, his early, puppy-love romance with Ashley, a deepening involvement with music, and, almost inevitably–given that his middle name had been inspired by Kobe Bryant–a turn toward basketball, at which he soon began to excel, which in turn led to a stint at Bryant's summer basketball camp in Santa Barbara, California, where he caught the attention of the Great One for the promise he showed on the court, and before long, when Tyler entered Erasmus High School in Flatbush, he wound up as a standout shooting guard on the JV team (freshman and sophomore years) and then the varsity as a junior and senior. The two Kobes were captured together in a memorable photograph from that summer in Santa Barbara, and how bitter it is to think that both of them are now dead, the older one on January twenty-sixth and the younger one on December twenty-third–at opposite ends of the dark, devastating year that was 2020.

He was an old soul in a young man's body, a quiet, contemplative person who spent much of his spare time alone, and yet Tyler matured so quickly in the last two years of his life that he became the moral center of the family. In spite of his age, he was the person the others turned to for advice, for help in solving problems and resolving conflicts because he was the one who could read human situations more clearly and impartially than anyone else. The heart of what he told them never varied: Be honest with yourself and others, act responsibly, do not blame others for your own faults or blunders, and if you stick to these principles, there's a good chance you will be able to overcome the impediments that stand before you. Ancient wisdom from the lips of a boy just barely into his twenties.

As one of his good friends said at the funeral service on January tenth, "Whatever I was going through, I could always talk to him . . . he was always there for me," and his older cousin Kareem went so far as to describe him as "a musician, a therapist, an athlete, an alleviator, and a role model." Some weeks later, during his conversation with Ostrander, he called Tyler "the sharpest edge of the family" and that "he absorbed everything." Almost in astonishment, he marveled at his cousin's sharp, "analytical mind" and the surge of inner growth that seemed to have transformed him in recent months. "Imagine a flower blooming before your eyes," he said, "and then someone comes along one day and clips the root from below."

Meanwhile, the family is still grieving. Tyler's mother and brother Shayne and girlfriend Ashley still talk about him in the present tense, as if he were hiding out somewhere in one of the rooms of the house. Tyler's empty boots continue to stand within breathing distance of the bed he shared with Ashley, and she has turned her dressing table into a small shrine of their life together, with an assemblage of photographs and numerous intimate, personal artifacts. The life-size cutout photograph of Tyler that stood by the chapel entrance on the day of the funeral now stands on the ground floor of the house. He is there with them still—there and yet not there—as his image and the memory of that image continue to reign over the ravaged household.

One wants to howl forth curses at the injustice of it all, but what judge can we turn to at such a time, and what human or extra-human force can put the scales of justice back in balance? The skies are silent. The earth is silent. Not even the most powerful god can undo what has already been done.

He was the homebody of the clan, the one who famously never wanted to go out to do anything that was not strictly necessary, but on the evening of December twenty-third he decided to break the pattern and leave the house with his brother Shayne to have his hair cut at Leroy's Barbershop on Church Avenue. That night, he would be attending the birthday party of one of his closest friends, there would be Christmas Eve dinner the following night, and the day after that would be Christmas, with the whole family gathered on the ground floor celebrating in full force, and Tyler wanted to look his best for those Wednesday, Thursday, and Friday events. As it happened, he was in uncommonly good spirits that day, and a few hours before he left the house with Shayne, he began talking about how lucky his life had been so far and how many extraordinary opportunities he had been given, from fencing lessons to piano lessons to basketball camp to various trips to distant places, and though he was looking back that day, there was much to look forward to as well, since he had recently finished his studies at the School of Cooperative Technical Education (Coop Tech) and was now a licensed electrician, which would have opened the door to a lifetime of productive work, and before long he and Ashley no doubt would have been married, and as she continued her training as an assistant elementary school teacher, it is almost certain that a day would have come when they began to talk about starting a family.

How chilling it is in retrospect to remember that speech of gratitude and happiness and to realize that those words were spoken just hours before his death—when a perfect stranger jumped out of a car and saw fit to end Tyler Kobe Nichols's brief journey through life with three stab wounds into the front of his body and one into his back.

On the day of the funeral, Tyler's mother stood up in front of a room crammed with mourners and openly confessed her grief and how difficult it was to bear, but she did not talk in anger against the unknown boy who had killed her son and did not call for revenge. She simply said, "I promise you one thing: Tyler's name will never be forgotten." After an anguished pause, she went on: "Tyler was brought up in love," and his murderer "was not brought up in love," and one day she would like to meet that person and other lost boys from the street "to show them what love is." And then she announced that she was planning to start a foundation in her son's name called *Long Live King Kobe.*

Two months after Tyler's death, that foundation was up and running.

Any and all proceeds from the sale of this book will be donated to Sherma Chambers's cause.

—Paul Auster

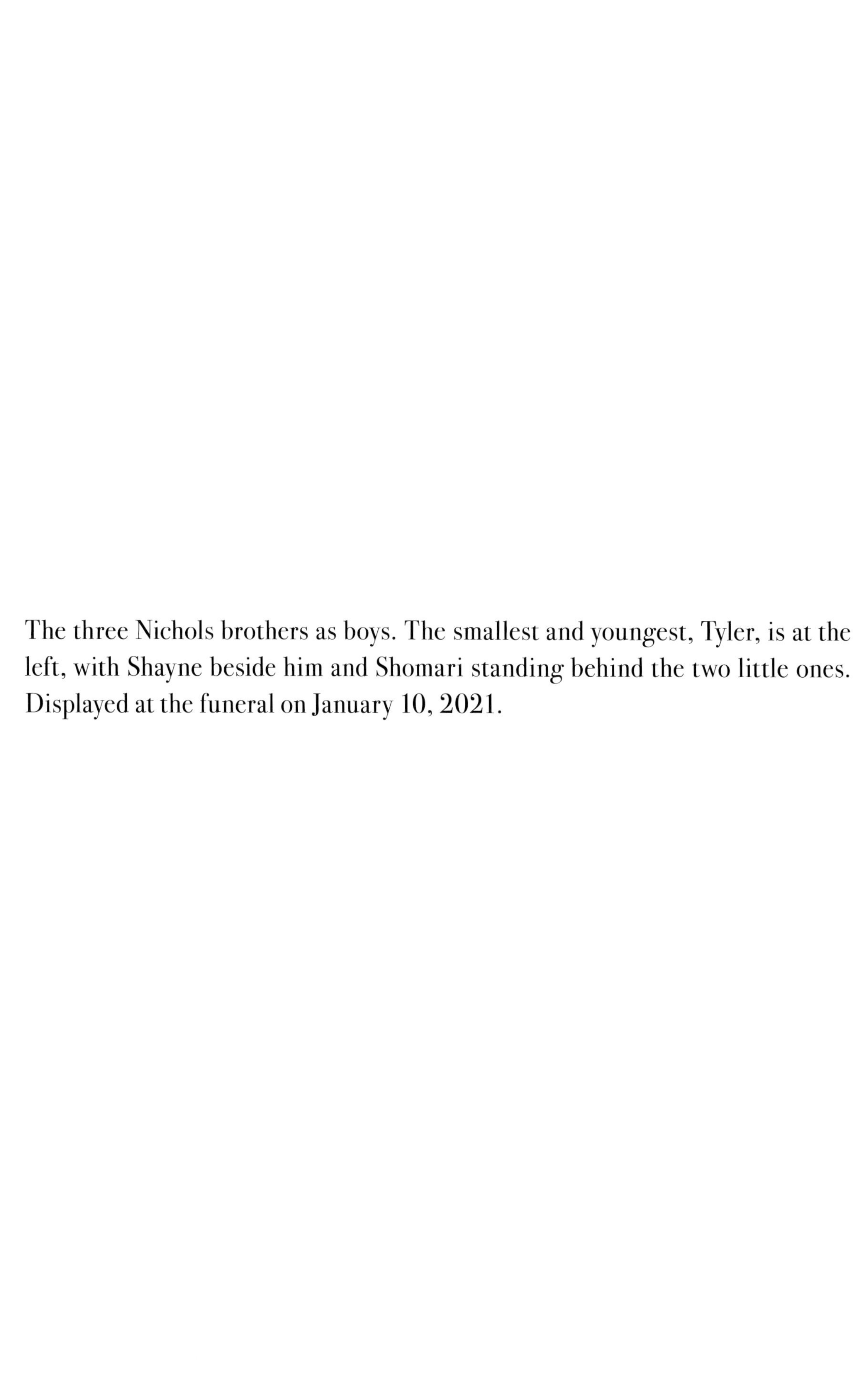

The three Nichols brothers as boys. The smallest and youngest, Tyler, is at the left, with Shayne beside him and Shomari standing behind the two little ones. Displayed at the funeral on January 10, 2021.

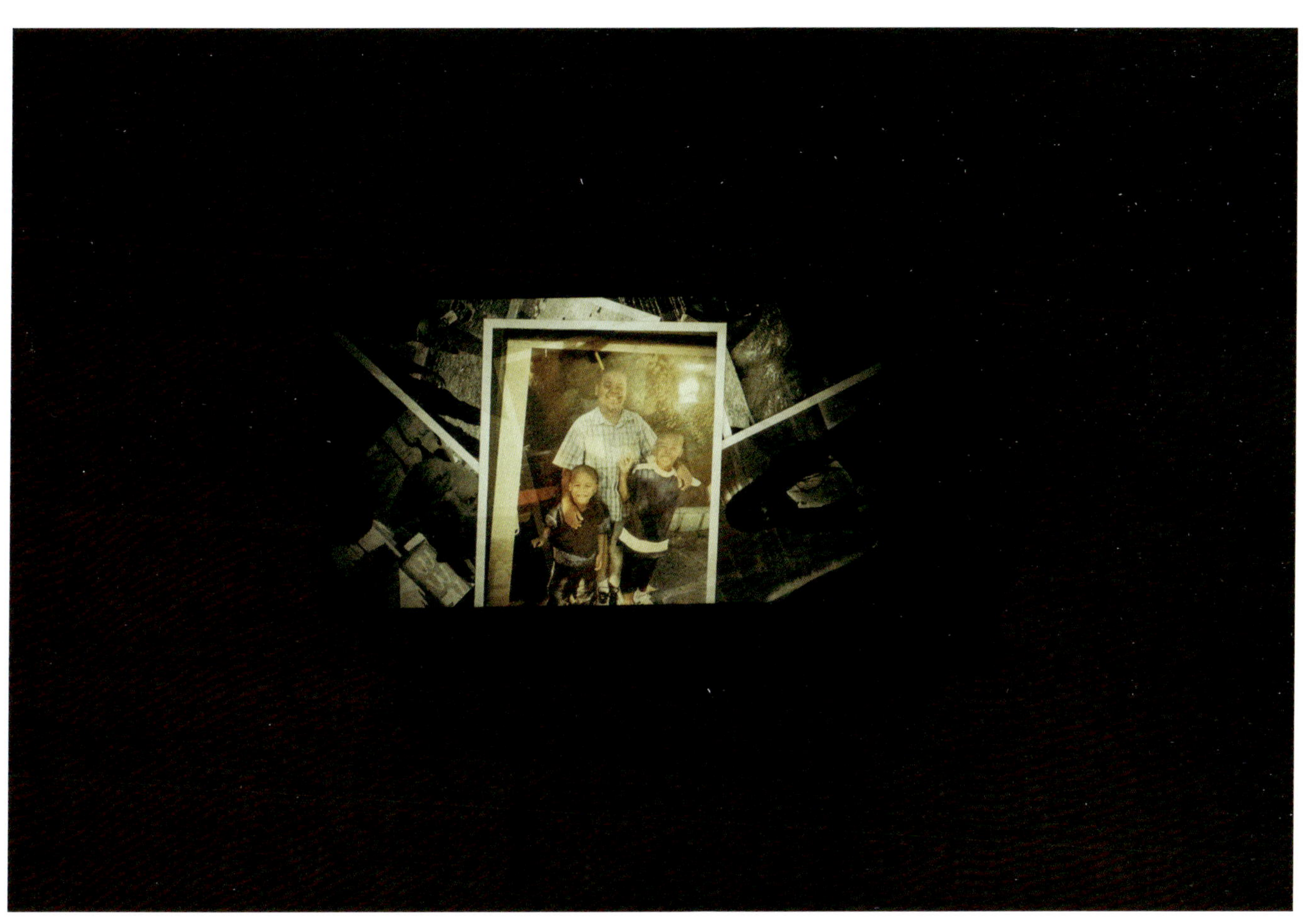

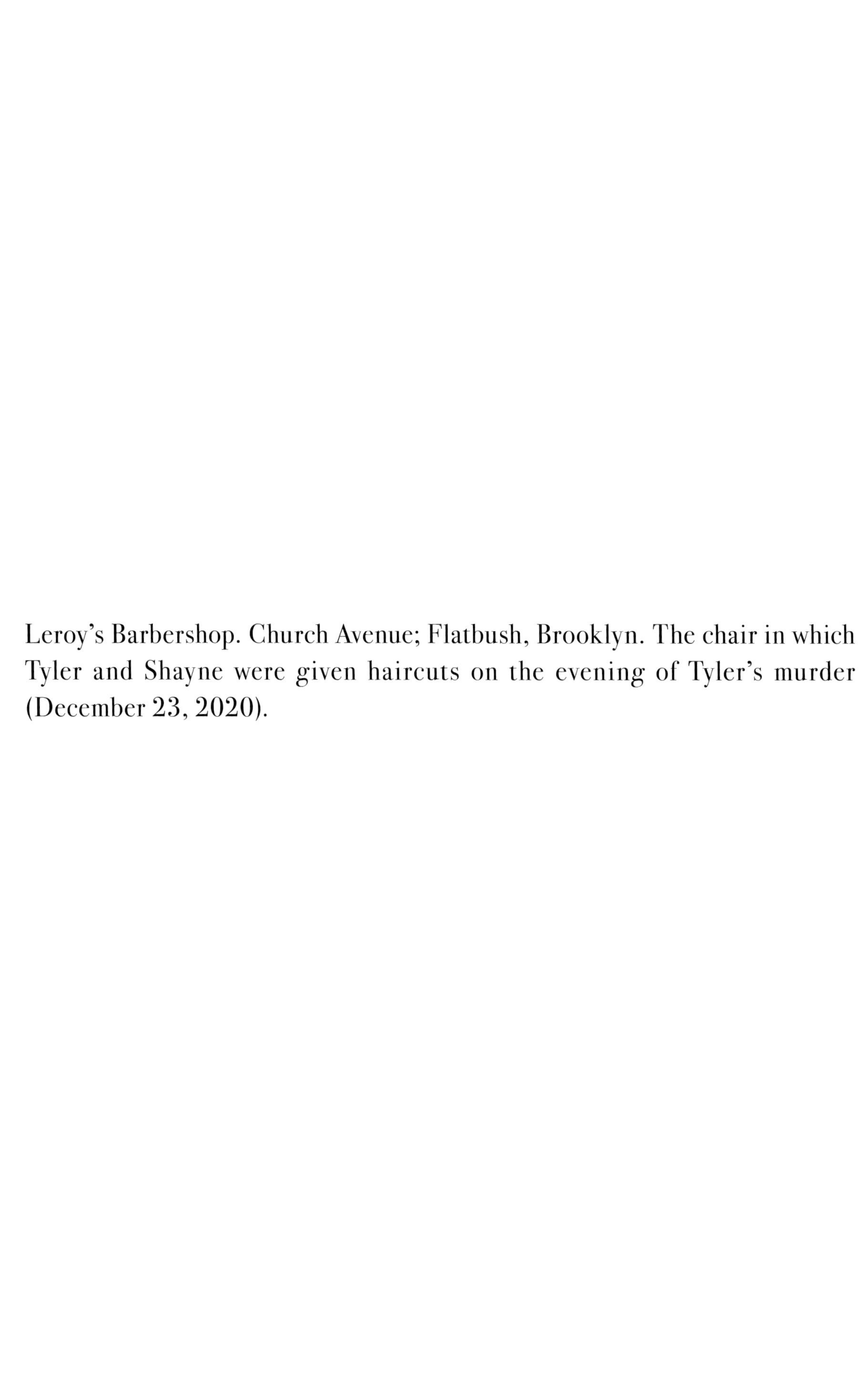

Leroy's Barbershop. Church Avenue; Flatbush, Brooklyn. The chair in which Tyler and Shayne were given haircuts on the evening of Tyler's murder (December 23, 2020).

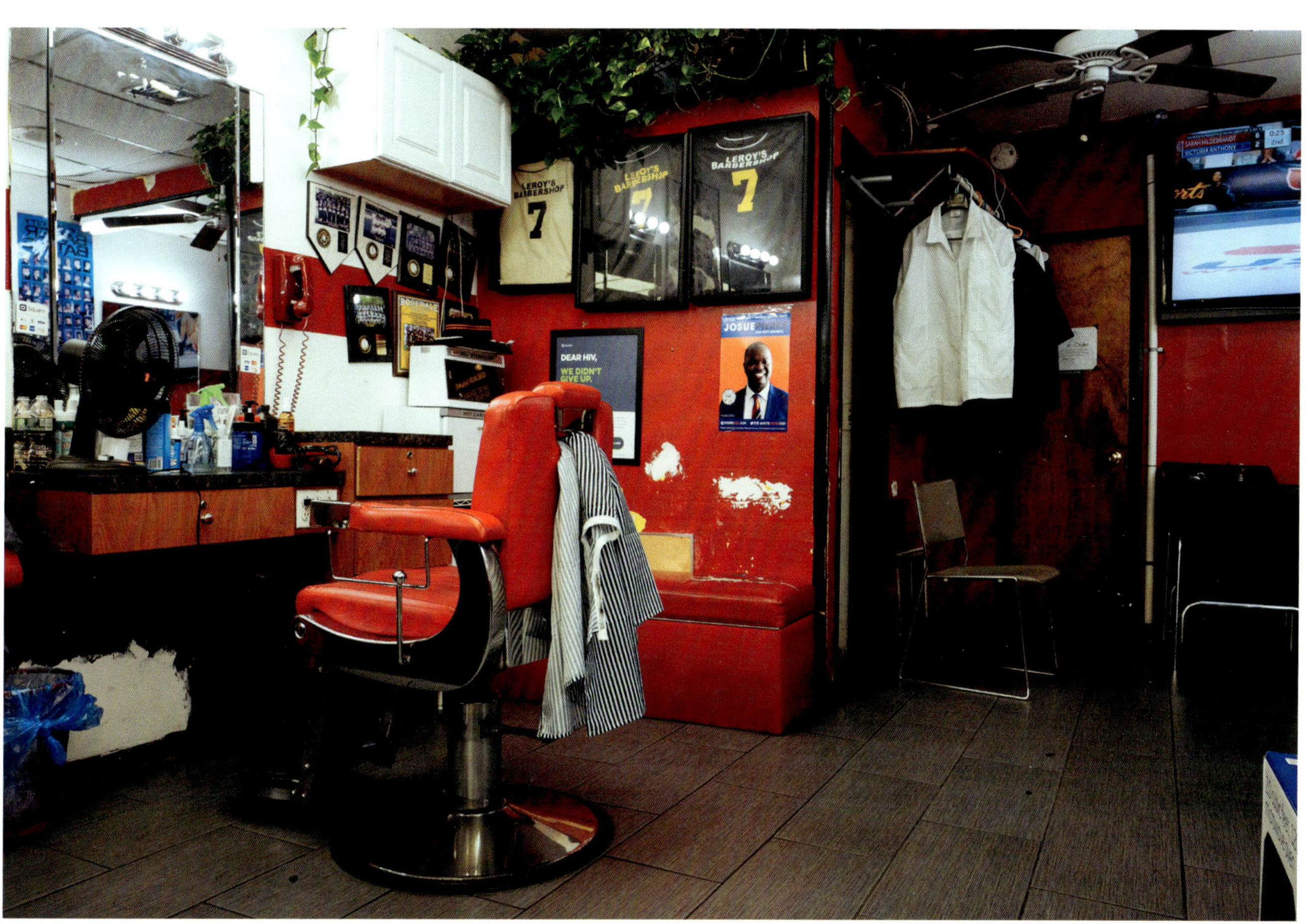
LEROY'S BARBERSHOP
7
LEROY'S BARBERSHOP
7
LEROY'S BARBERSHOP
7
DEAR HIV,
WE DIDN'T GIVE UP.
JOSUE
SARAH HILDEBRANDT
VICTORIA ANTHONY

The corner of Coney Island Avenue and Turner Place: the site of the attack on the two Nichols brothers by the five strangers.

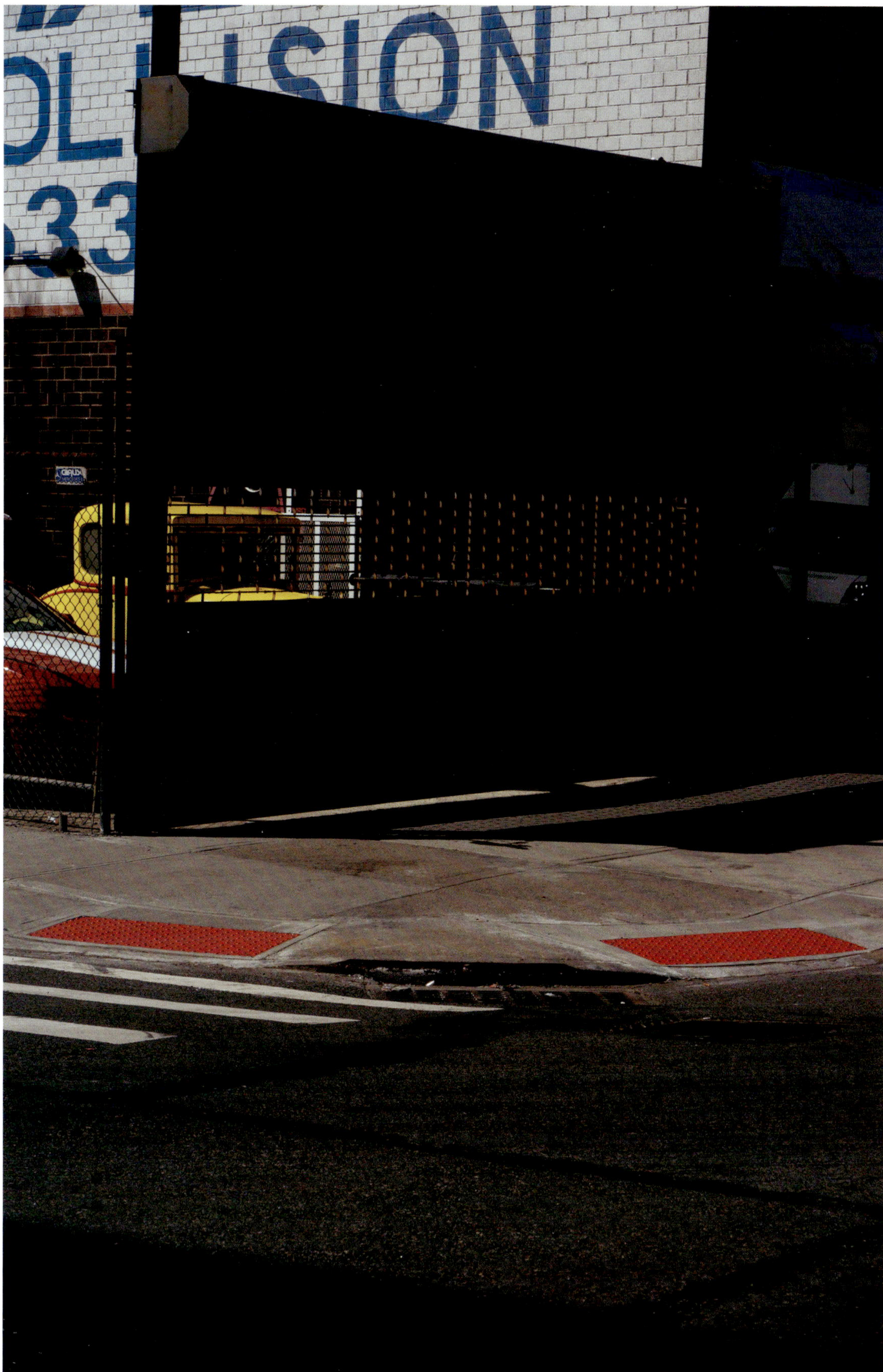
SION

After the five attackers left the scene, Tyler and Shayne began heading home, but the mortally wounded Tyler could make it no farther than to the corner of Turner Place and East 8th Street, just half a block from where the brothers lived. Tyler collapsed on this corner, which is where the ambulance arrived after the 911 call.

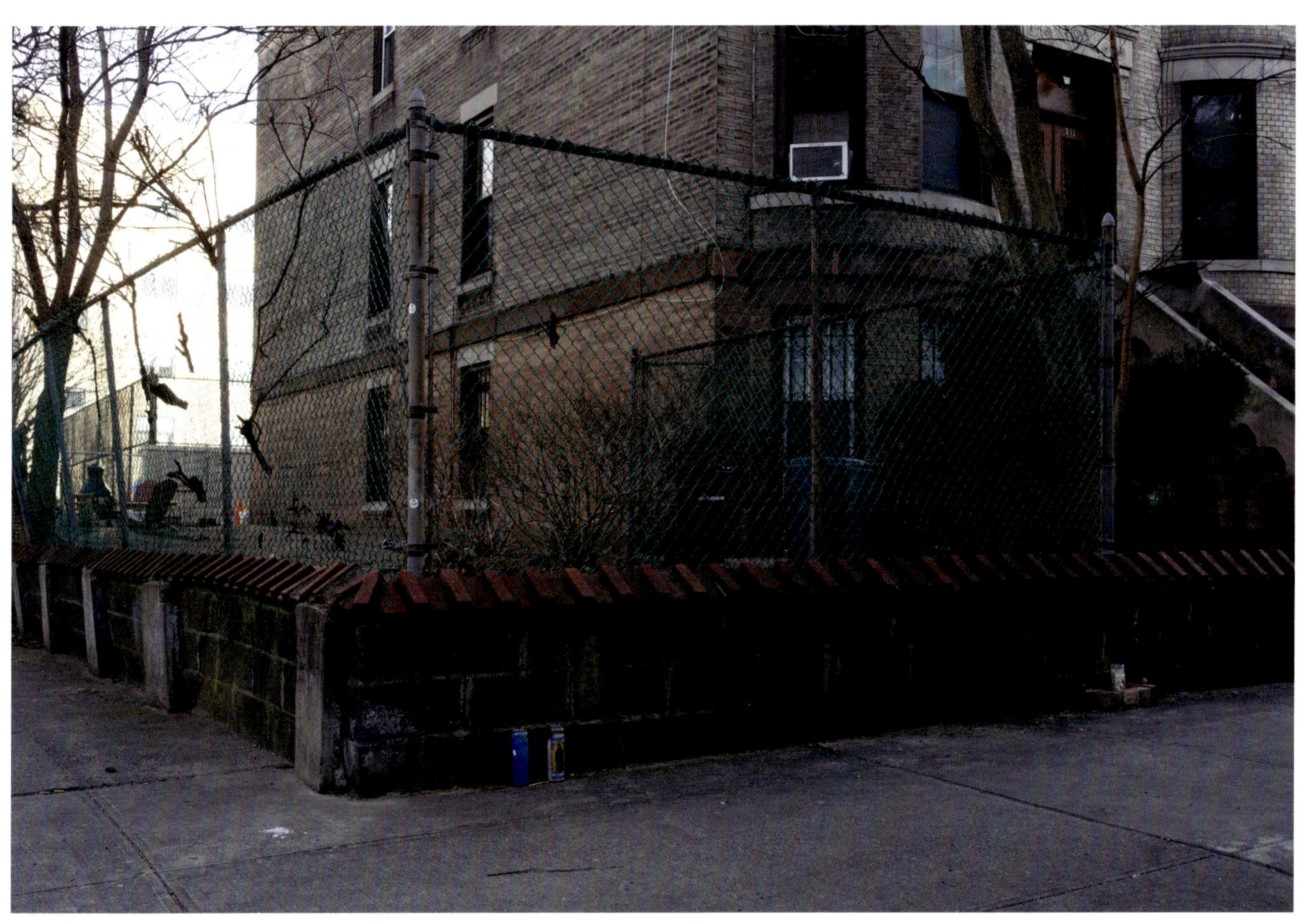

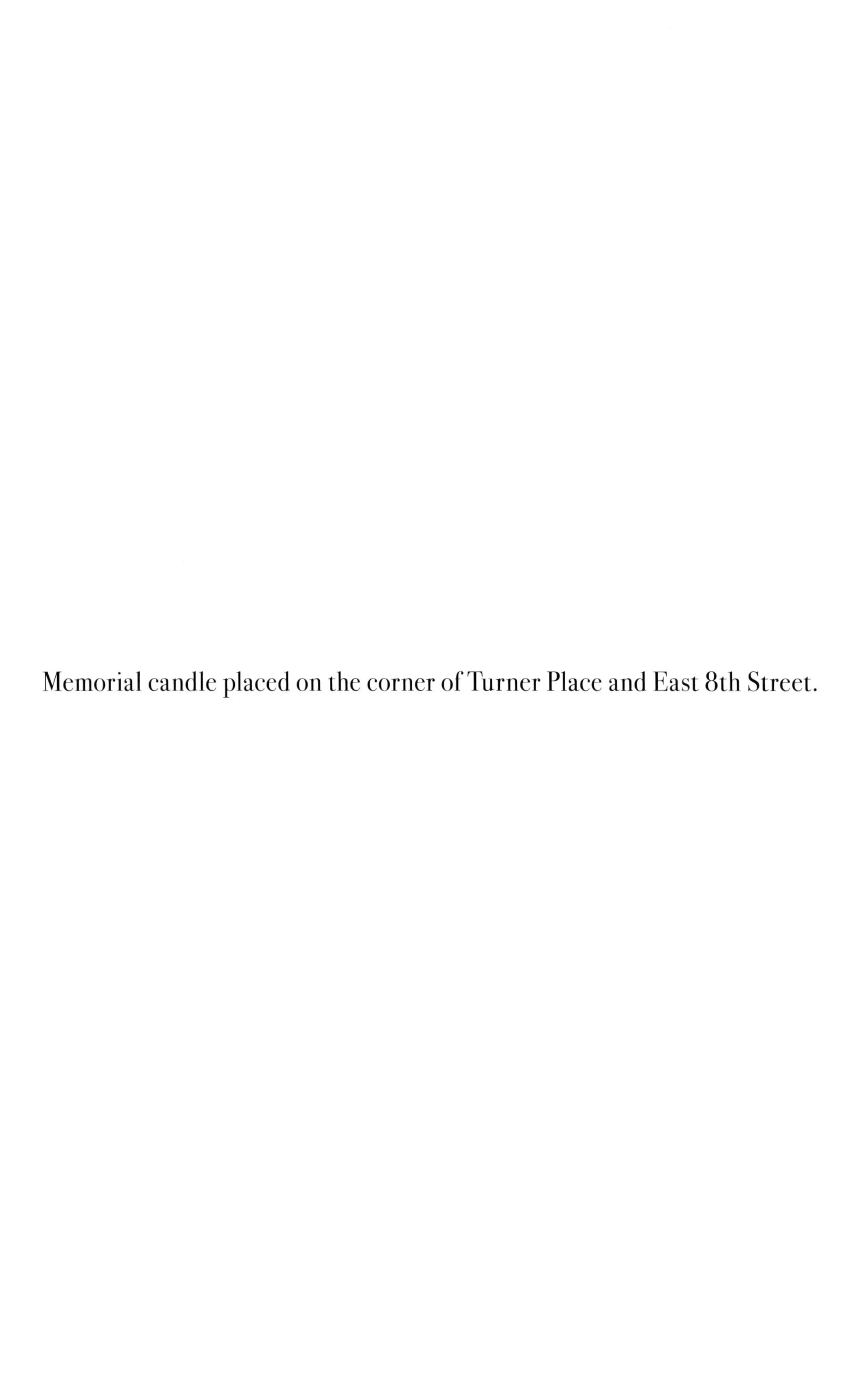

Memorial candle placed on the corner of Turner Place and East 8th Street.

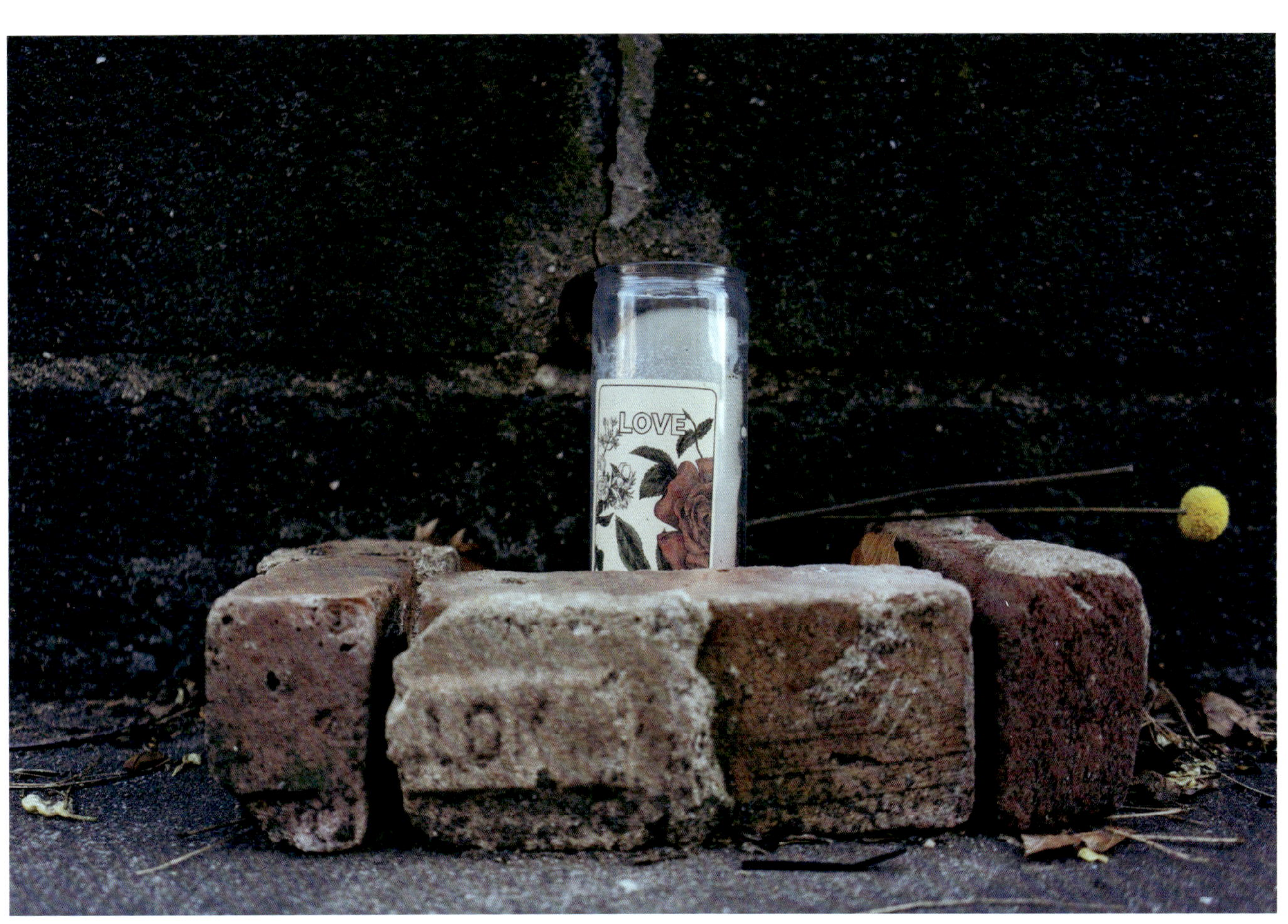
LOVE

Security camera jutting from the side of P.S. 889 on the corner of Coney Island Avenue and Turner Place. The attack of the five strangers against the two brothers was recorded on this camera and led to the arrest of the accused killer, but the police have not yet disclosed any of the pictures documenting the crime.

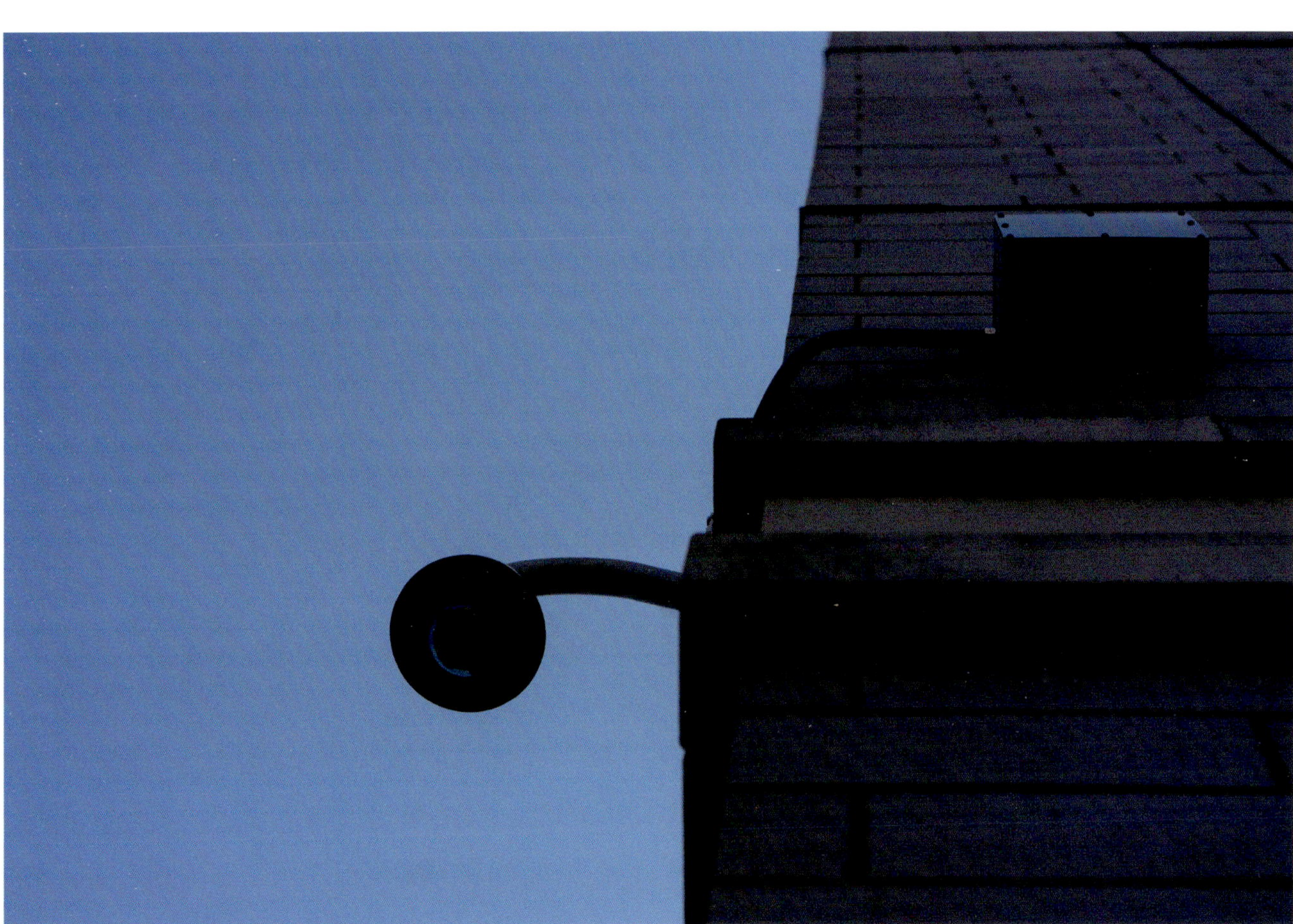

Harmony Funeral Home, January 8, 2021, as preparations were being made for the service on the 10th.

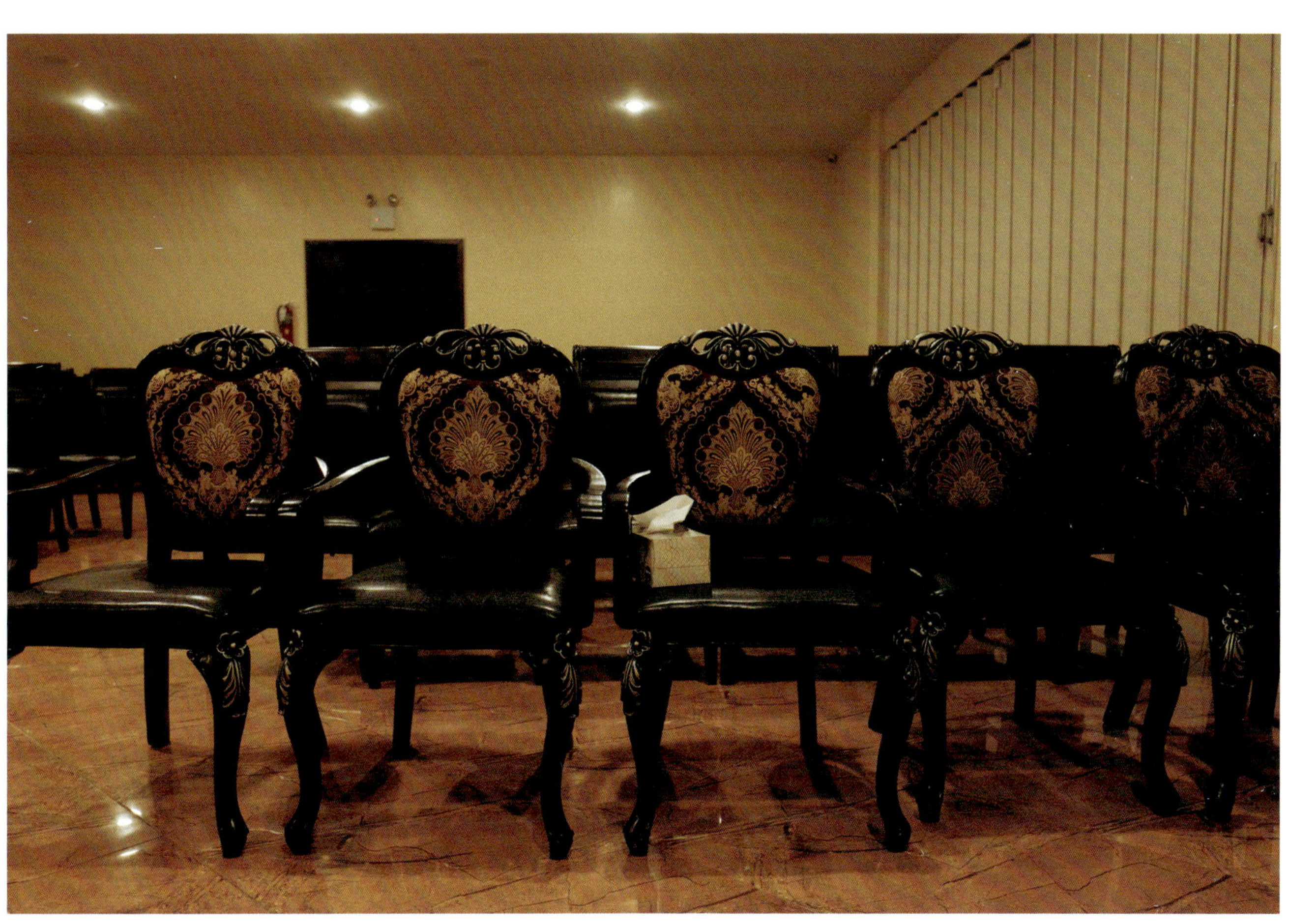

Empty hallway at Harmony Funeral Home; January 8, 2021.

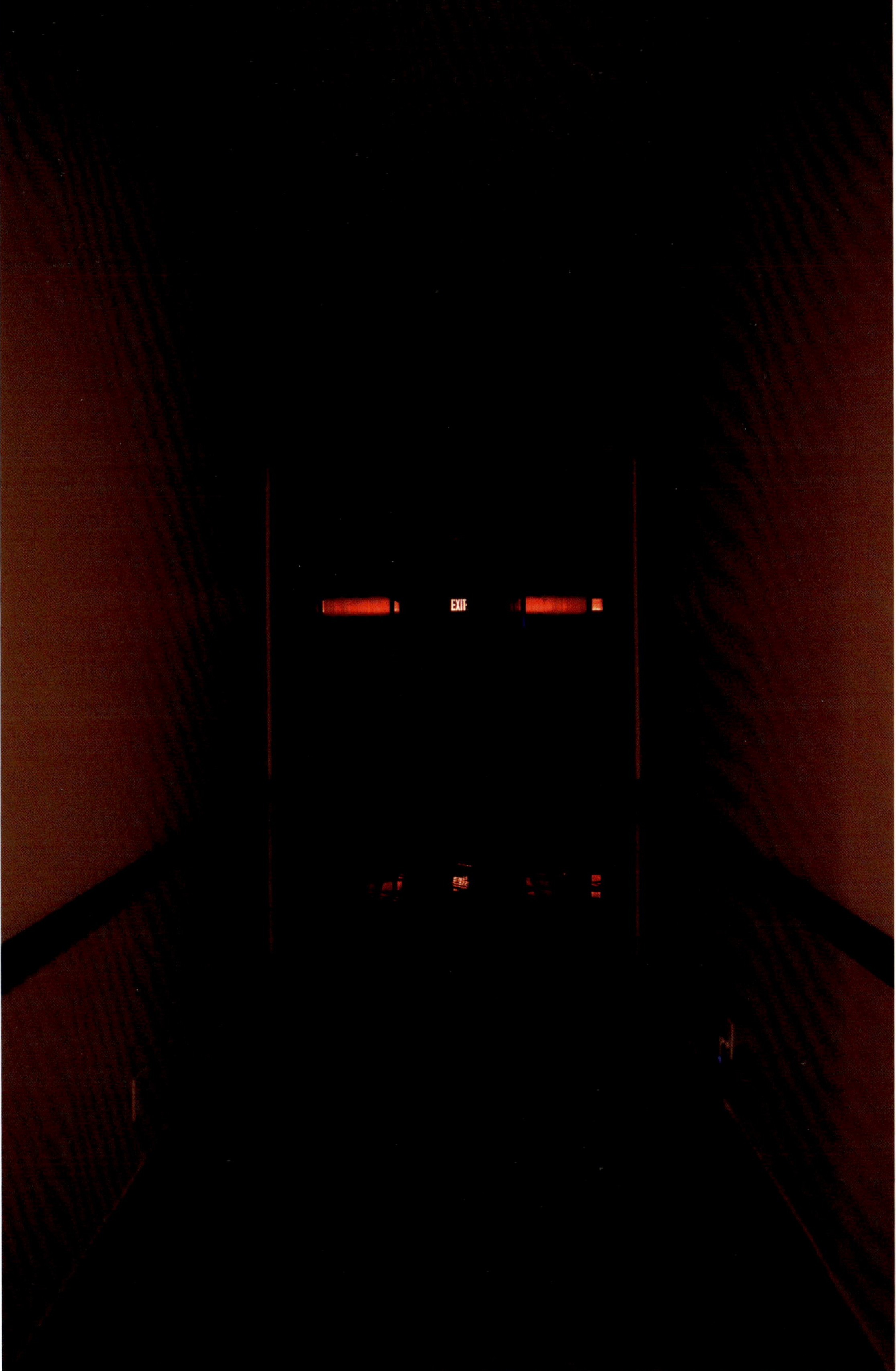
EXIT

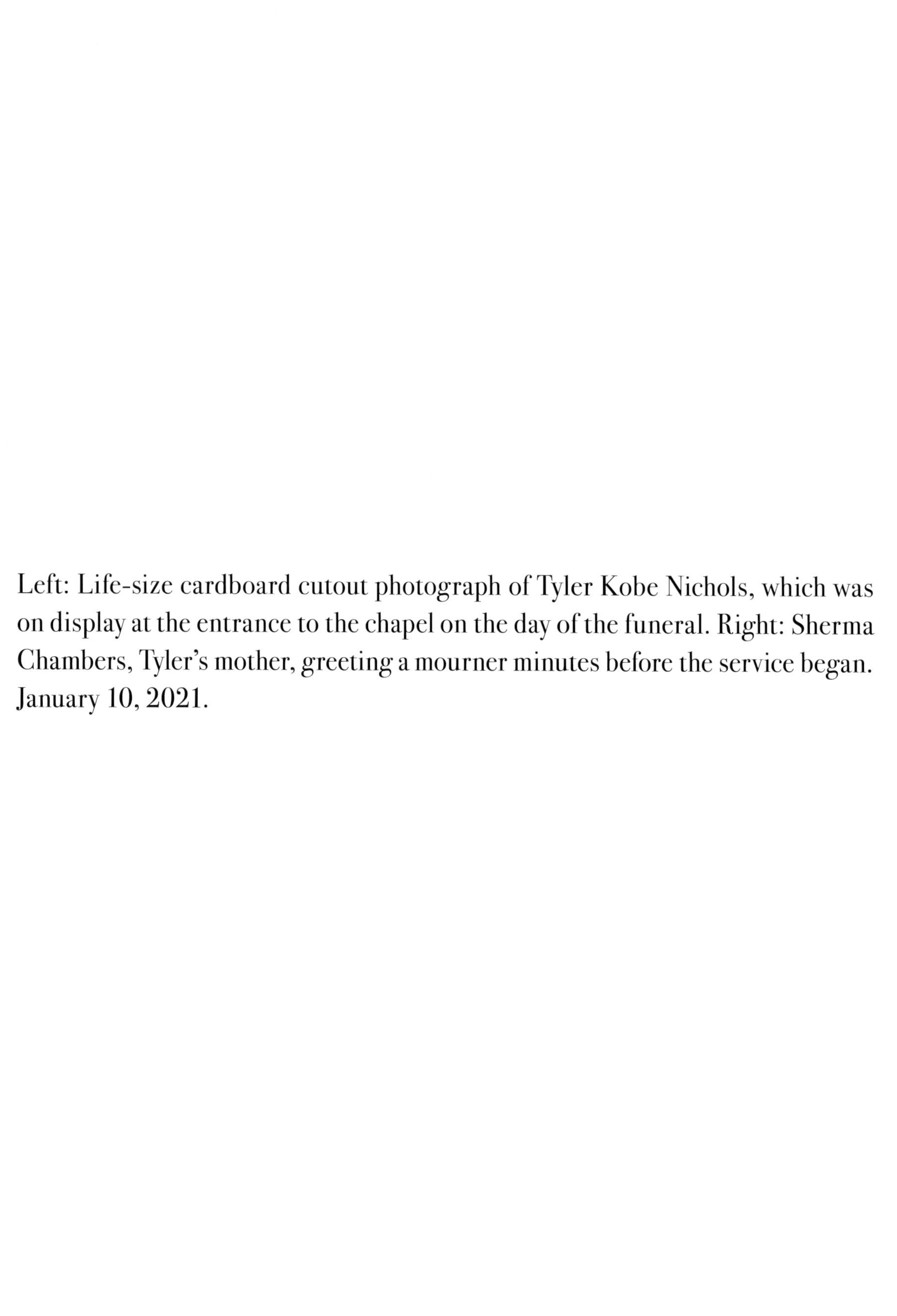

Left: Life-size cardboard cutout photograph of Tyler Kobe Nichols, which was on display at the entrance to the chapel on the day of the funeral. Right: Sherma Chambers, Tyler's mother, greeting a mourner minutes before the service began. January 10, 2021.

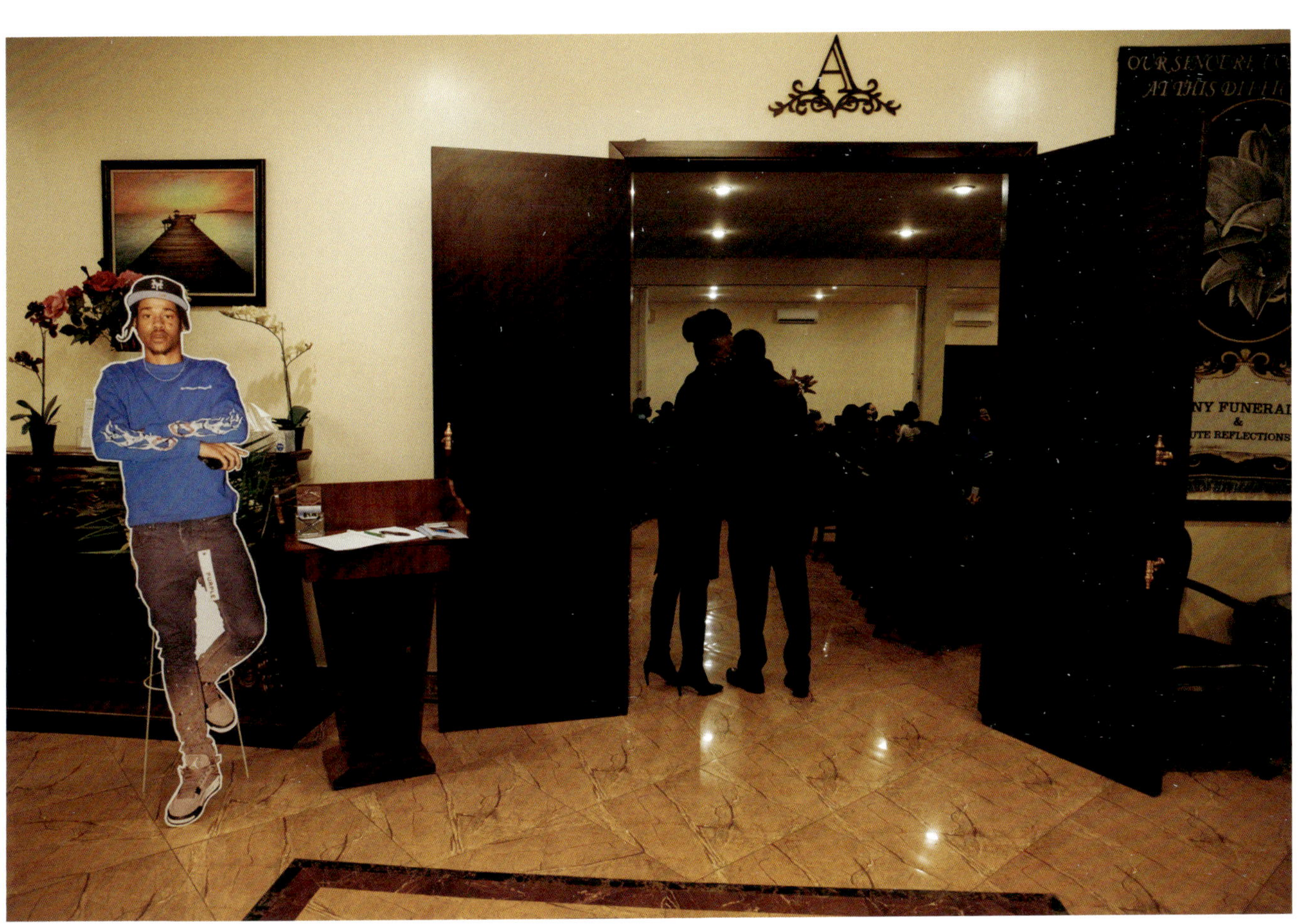

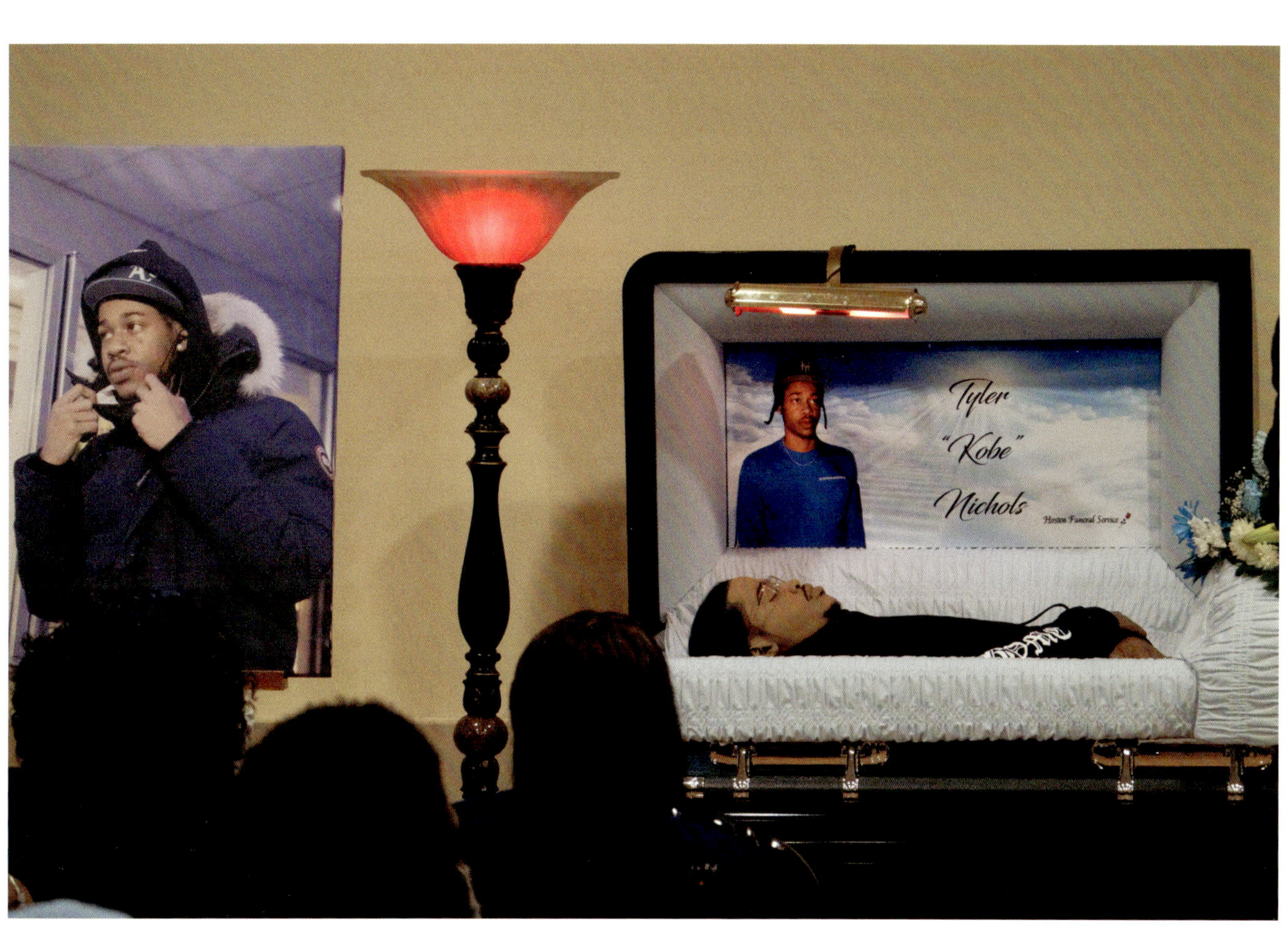
Tyler
"Kobe"
Nichols

Sherma Chambers with Ashley Duverneau (Tyler's girlfriend) to her right and Brittany Augustine (Shayne's girlfriend) to her left.

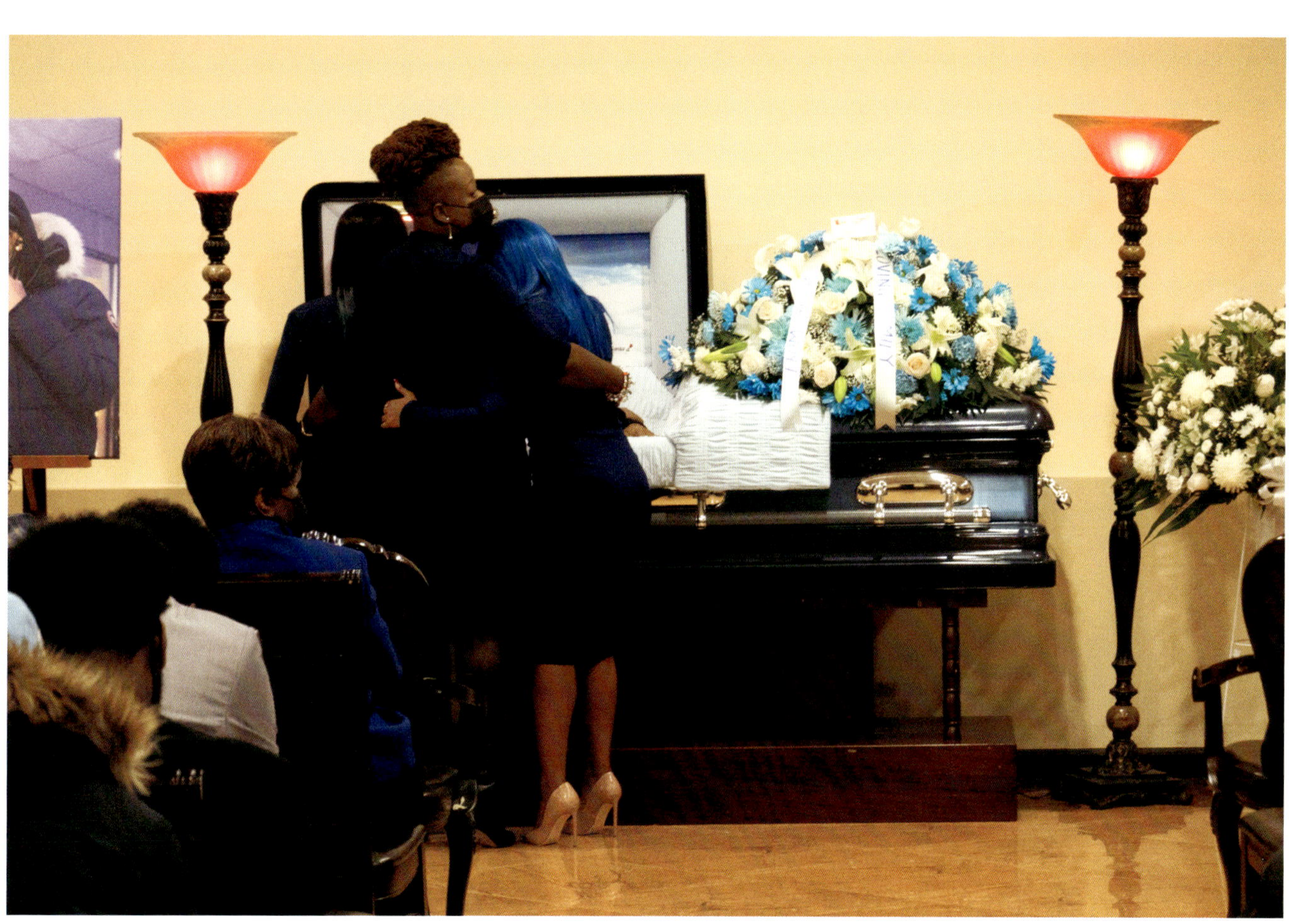

Tyler's friends.

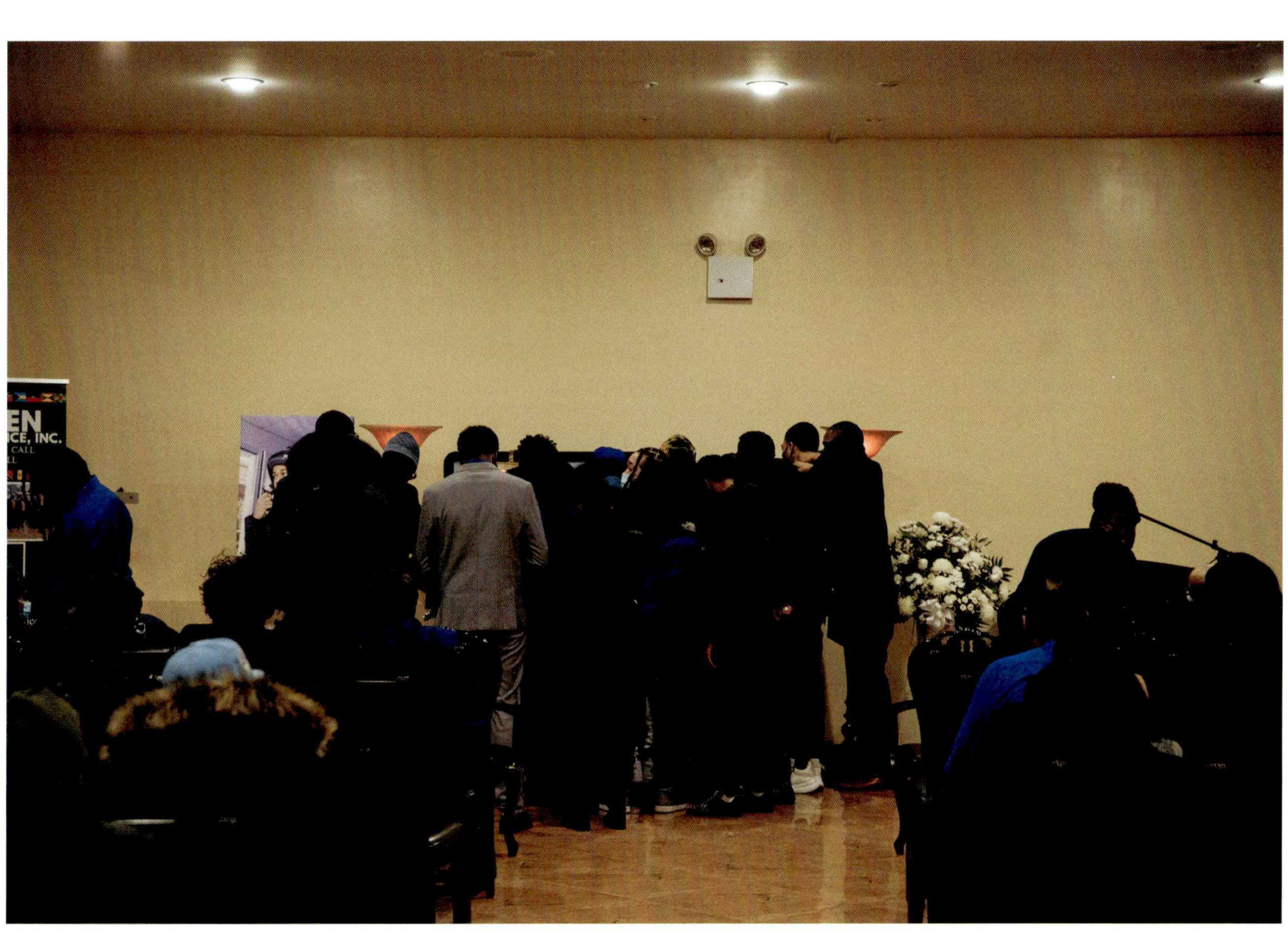

Photograph displayed at the funeral showing Tyler and some of his friends in the backyard of his house. Tyler, shirtless, is standing in the middle of the frame.

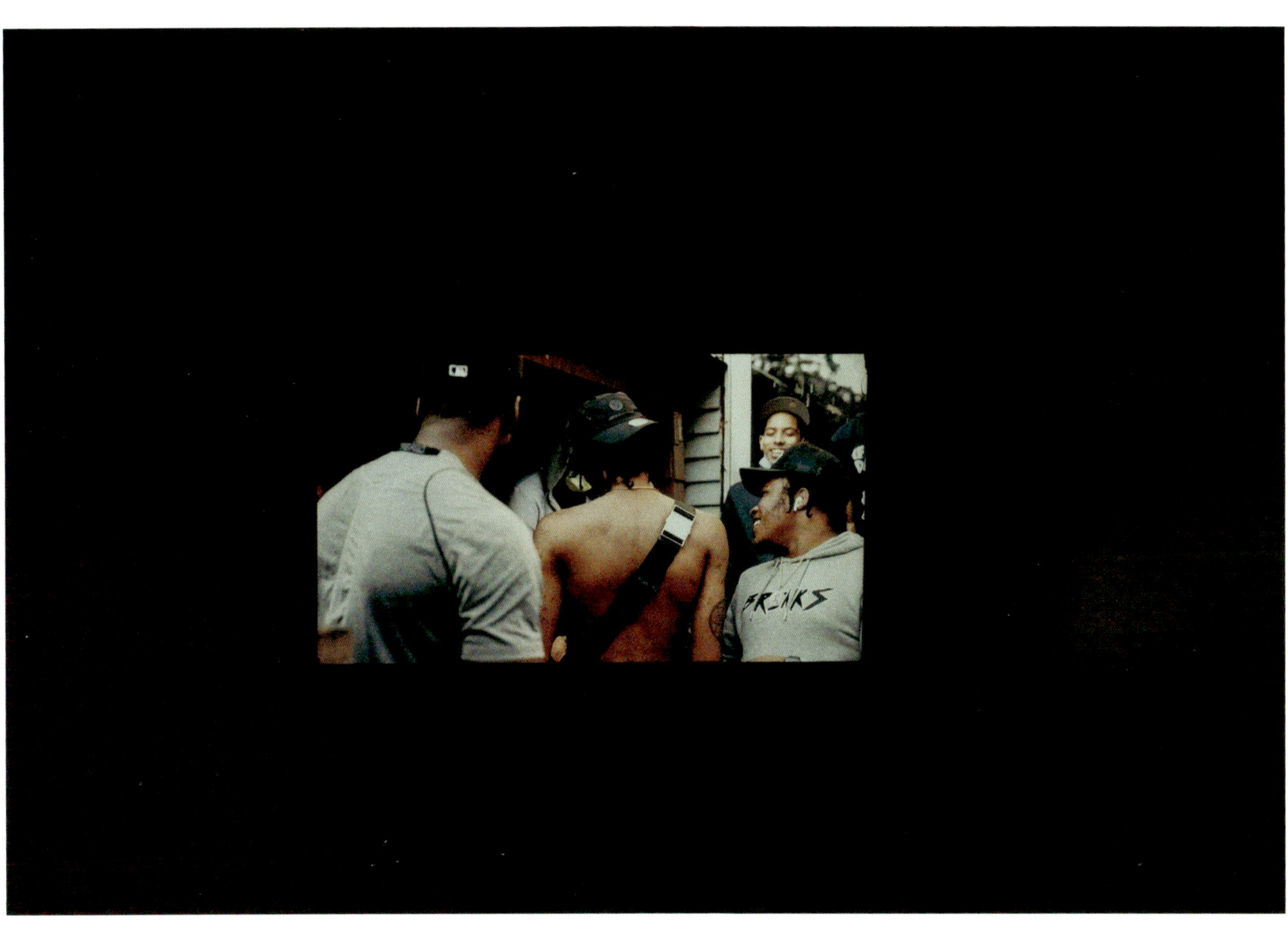

Memorial photograph of Tyler posted outside the family house. The hands touching the frame belong to his cousin Kareem Eusebe.

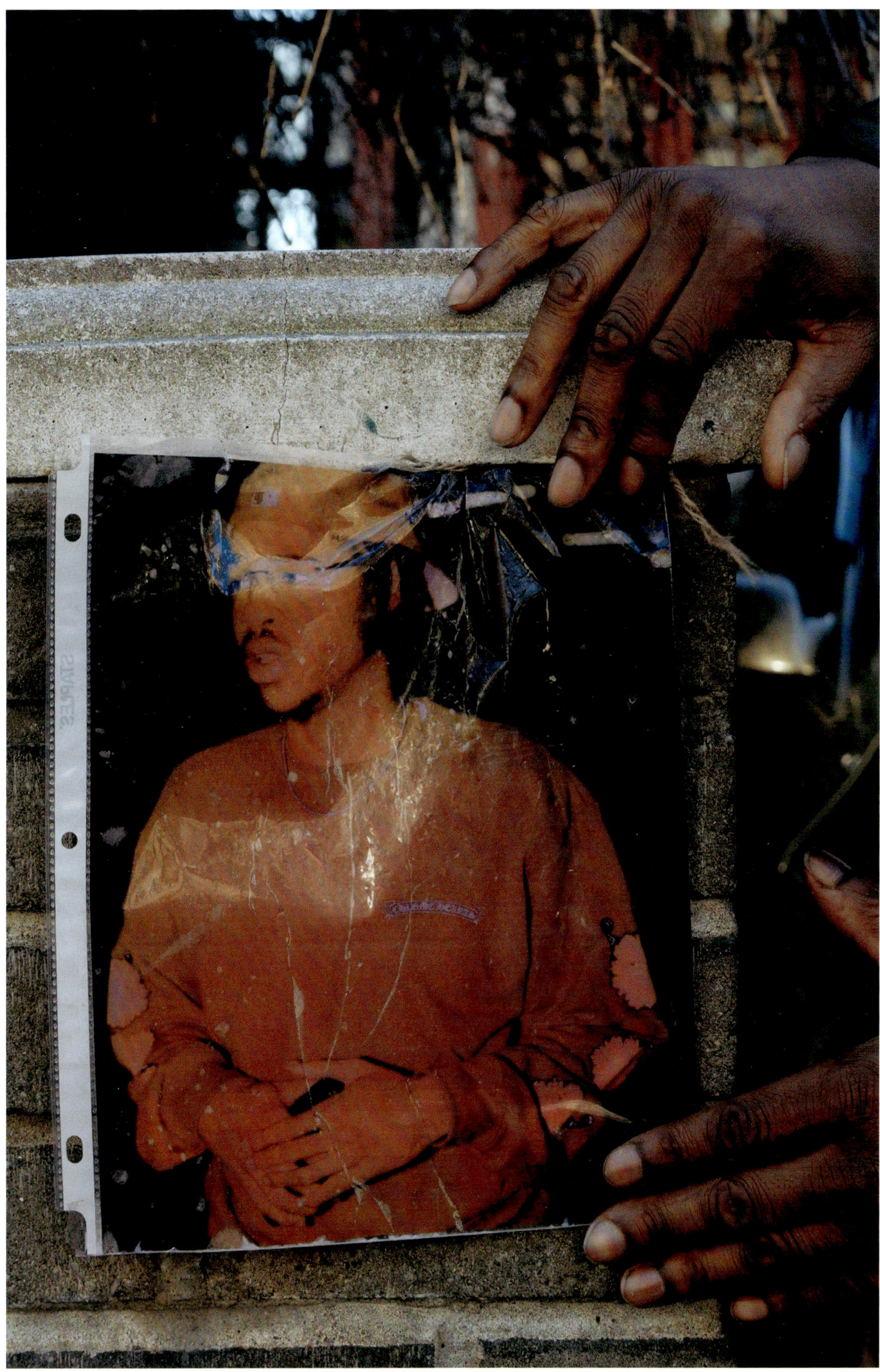

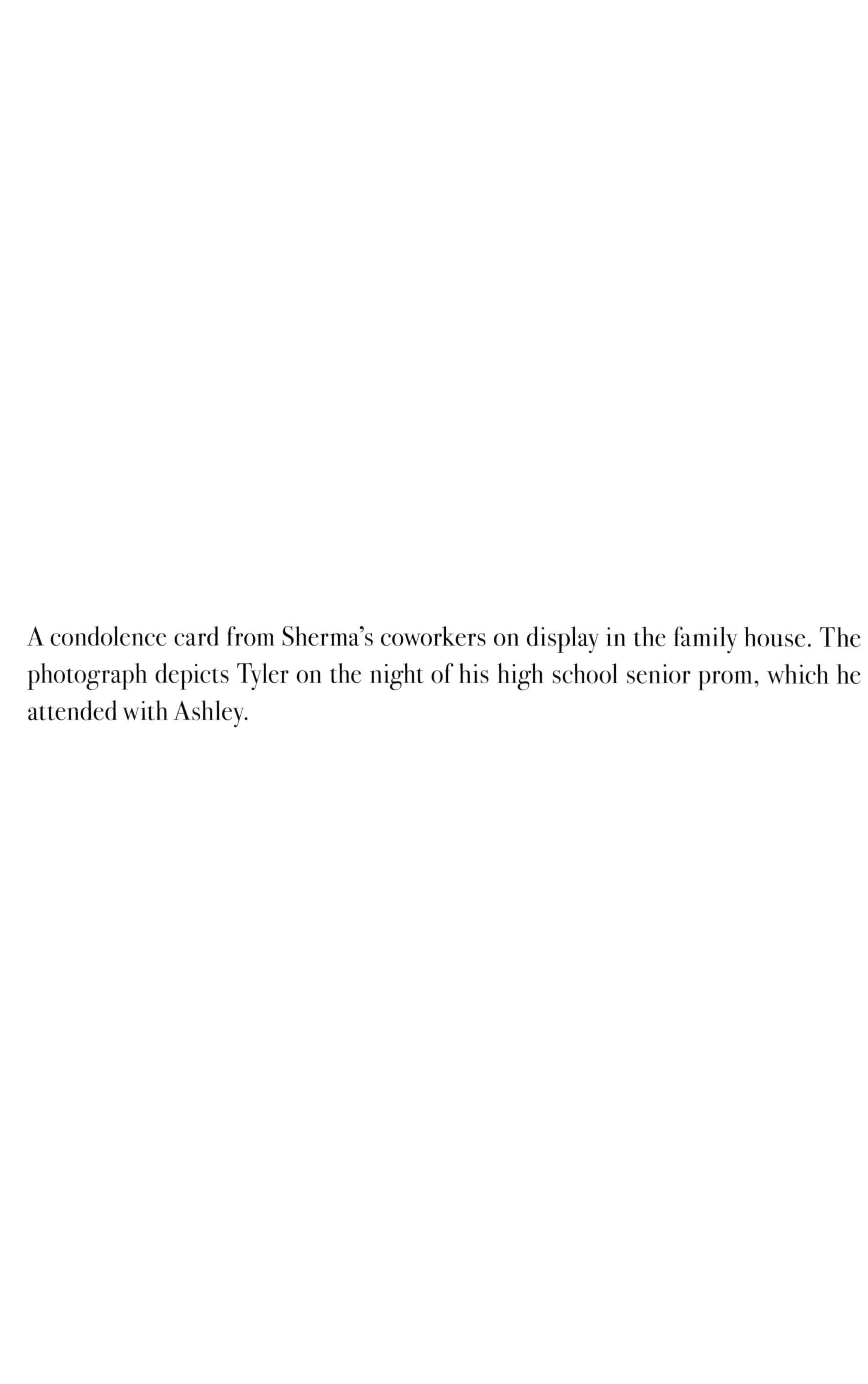

A condolence card from Sherma's coworkers on display in the family house. The photograph depicts Tyler on the night of his high school senior prom, which he attended with Ashley.

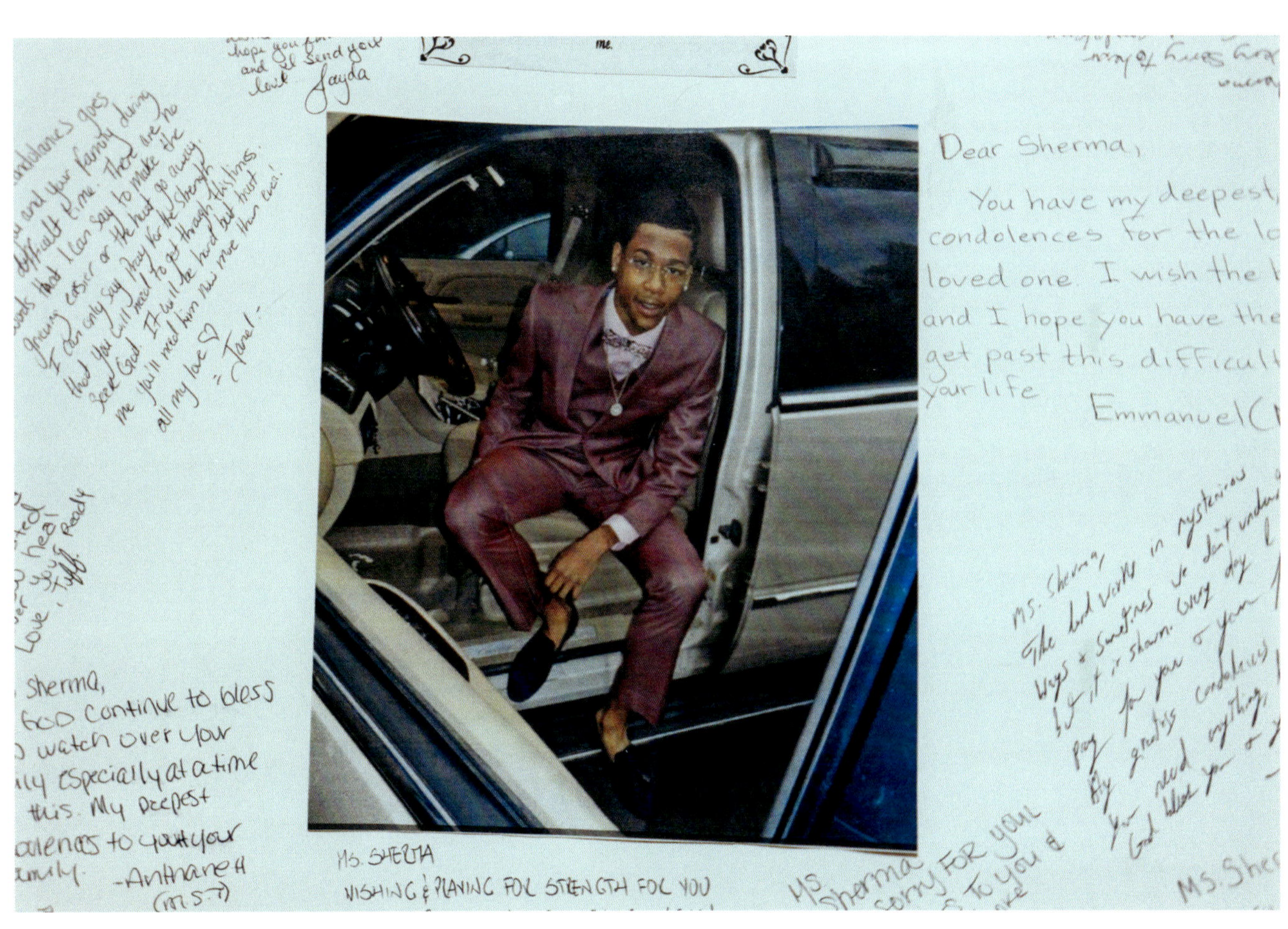

Dear Sherma,
You have my deepest
condolences for the lo
loved one. I wish the
and I hope you have the
get past this difficult
your life
Emmanuel
Sherma,
GOD continue to bless
watch over your
especially at a time
this. My deepest
to your
-Anthane H
MS. SHERMA
WISHING & PRAYING FOR STRENGTH FOR YOU
Jayda

Sherma Chambers at home; January 28, 2021.

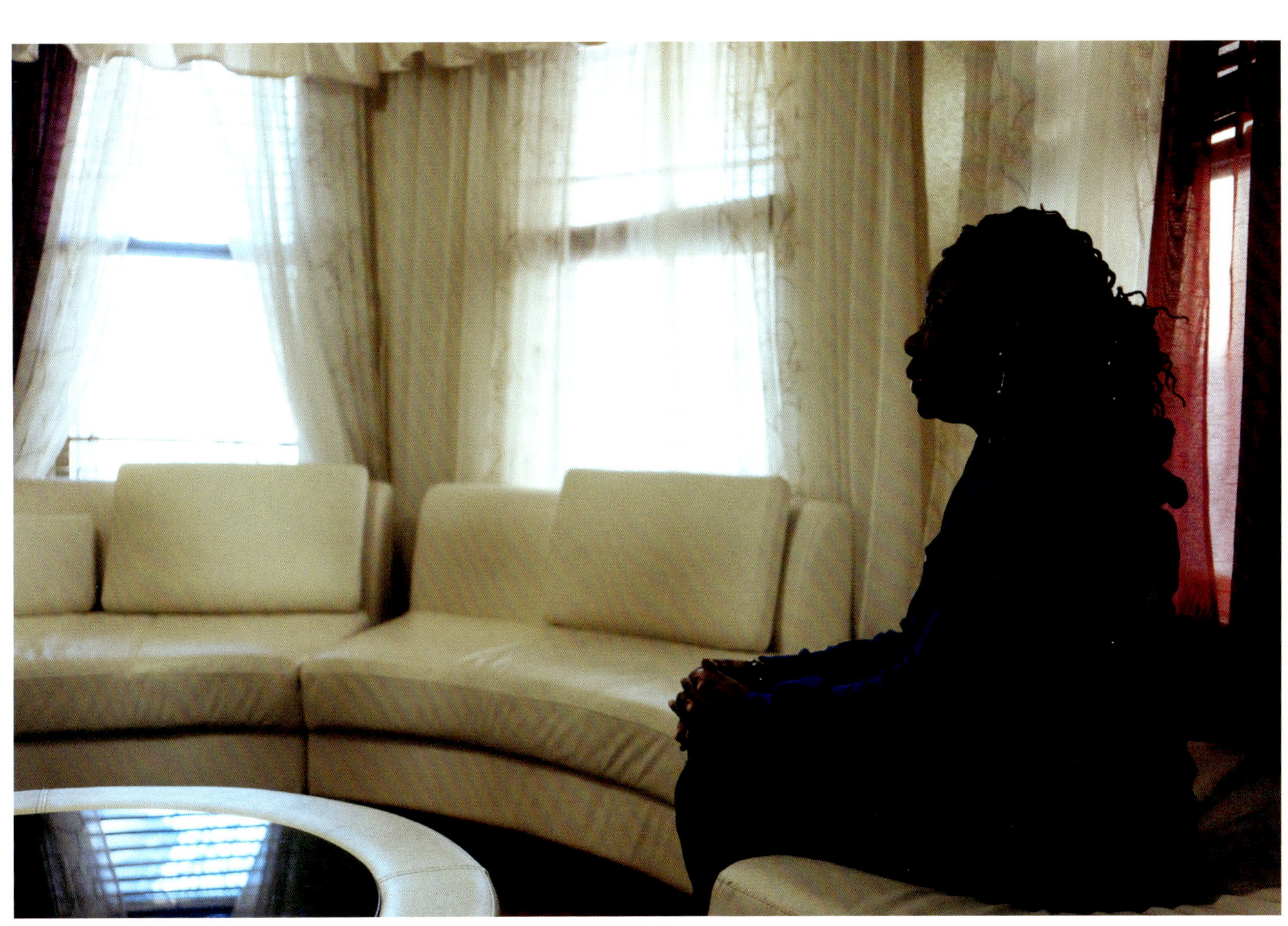

Shayne Nichols; January 28, 2021.

5/1/21. Kareem Eusebe, first cousin of the Nichols brothers, reports that as Tyler and Shayne were heading home from the barbershop on the night of the killing, they crossed Coney Island Avenue at Turner Place and walked between the two cars occupied by the five strangers just before they reached the corner on the other side of the street. Shayne glanced into one of the cars for a brief moment while passing by, and no more than seconds after that, as he and Tyler continued walking down the sidewalk, the person sitting on the passenger side of the double-parked car jumped out and threw a punch at Shayne. Tyler retaliated by throwing a punch at Shayne's attacker, and almost at once the person sitting on the driver's side of the double-parked car leapt out, ran to the sidewalk, and stabbed Tyler in the back, piercing his lung. Gravely wounded, Tyler nevertheless fought on as the five strangers swarmed around the two brothers and went after them with their fists. Before long, Shayne was down on the pavement, huddled up in what Kareem describes as a "fetal position." After a moment or two of hesitation, as if struggling to decide whether to back off or push forward and attack the person who had knocked Shayne to the ground, Tyler chose to push forward and attack. That was when the knife came out again and stabbed him three more times, once in the spleen, once in the liver, and once in the heart. The wounds were so precise and so devastating, Kareem says, that it was "like an orchestrated assassination."

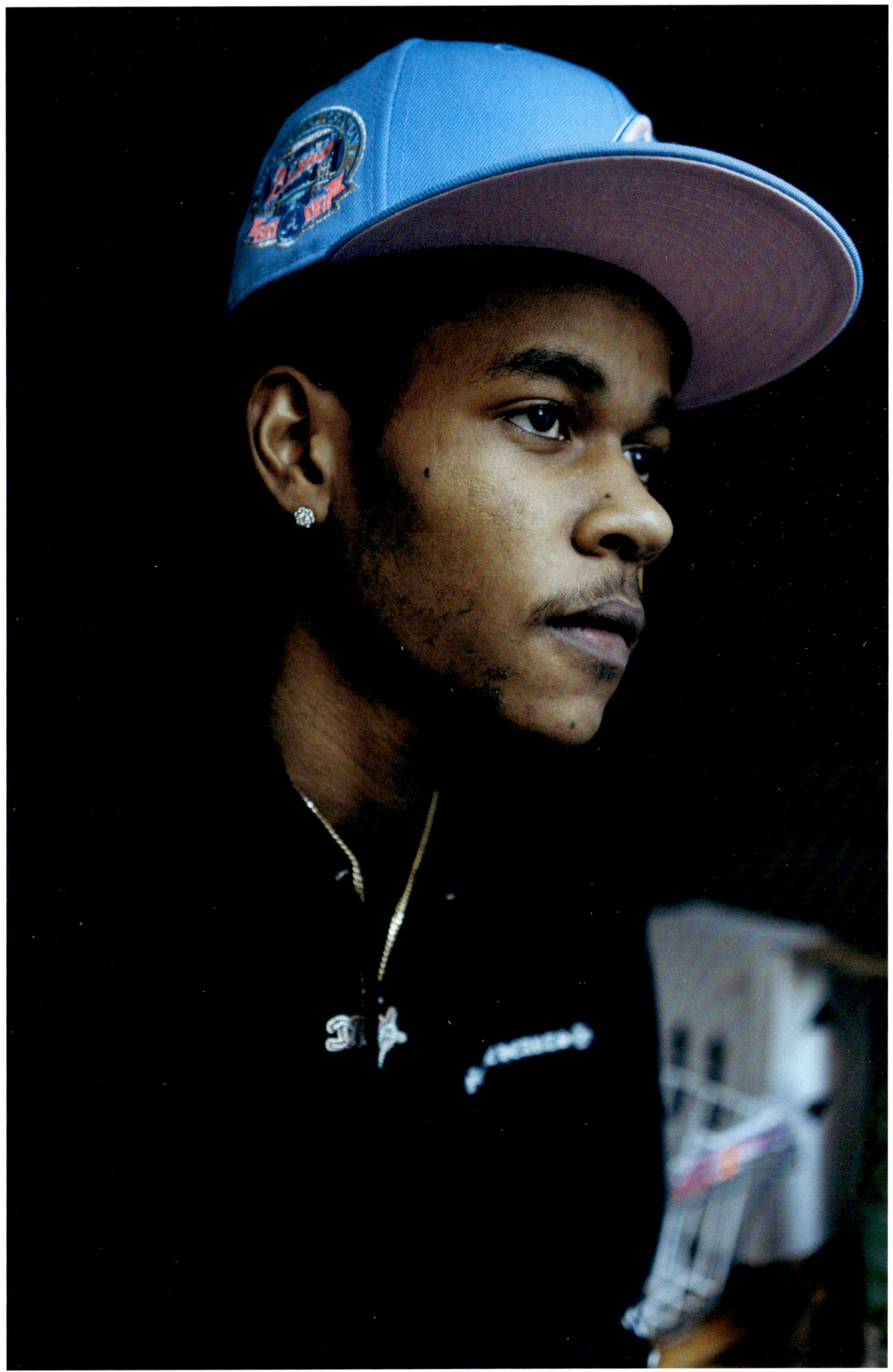

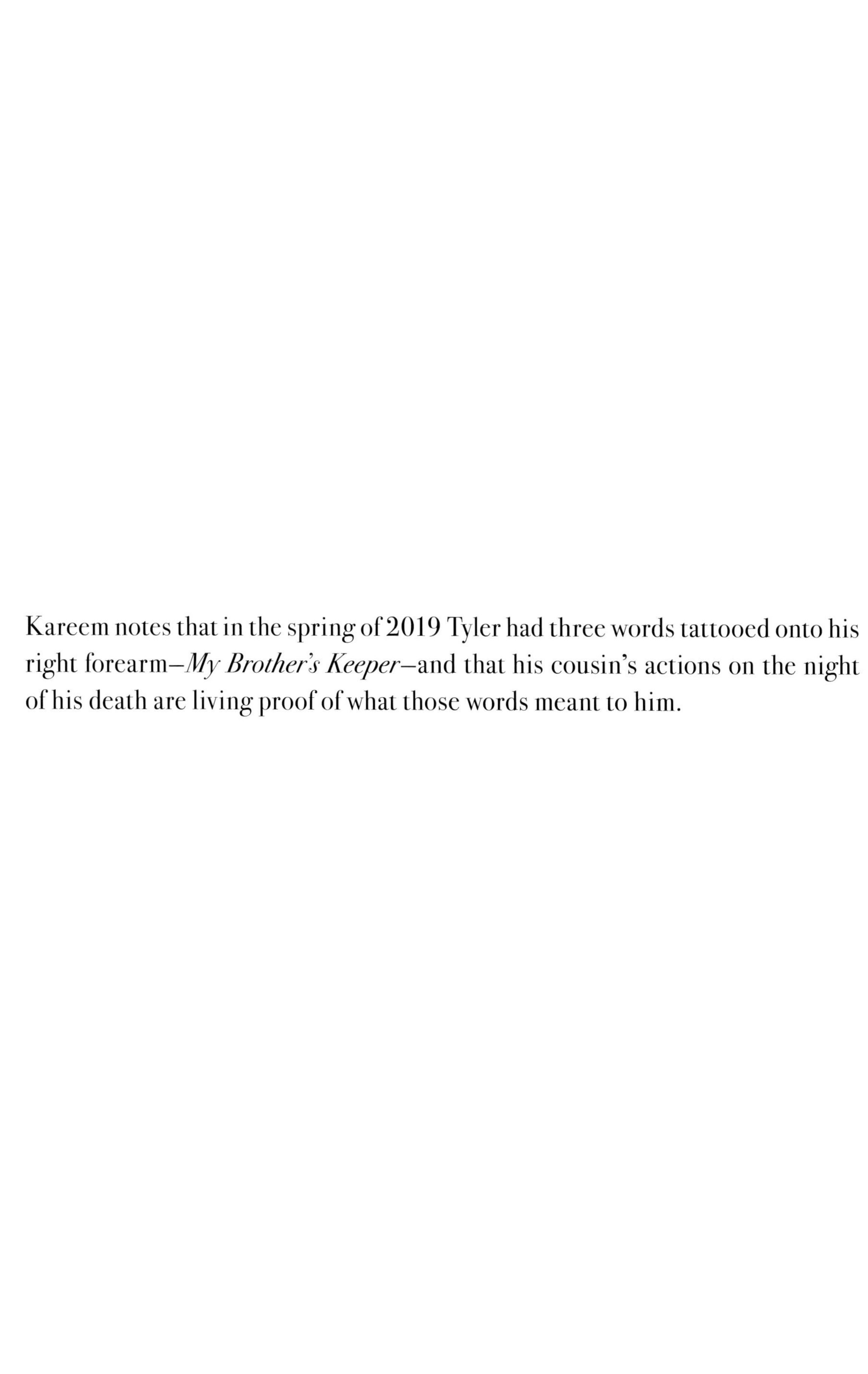

Kareem notes that in the spring of 2019 Tyler had three words tattooed onto his right forearm—*My Brother's Keeper*—and that his cousin's actions on the night of his death are living proof of what those words meant to him.

Kareem also notes that Shayne has been the hardest hit of anyone in the family by the events of that night, not only because he was involved in them and witnessed them with his own eyes, but because watching his brother die was no different from standing inside his brother's body and watching himself die.

Wanting to protect her sons from the dangers of the streets, even in the relative tranquility of their Kensington neighborhood, Sherma resolved to establish a household that would provide a safe haven for her boys and their schoolmates. More than a hospitable environment, the ground floor of the house evolved into a miniature community center for Shayne and Tyler's closest friends, and the extended Nichols-Chambers family was extended still further to include various outsiders, who in the end became insiders as well. All the young men and women who became part of that intimate, inner circle addressed Sherma as Mommy.

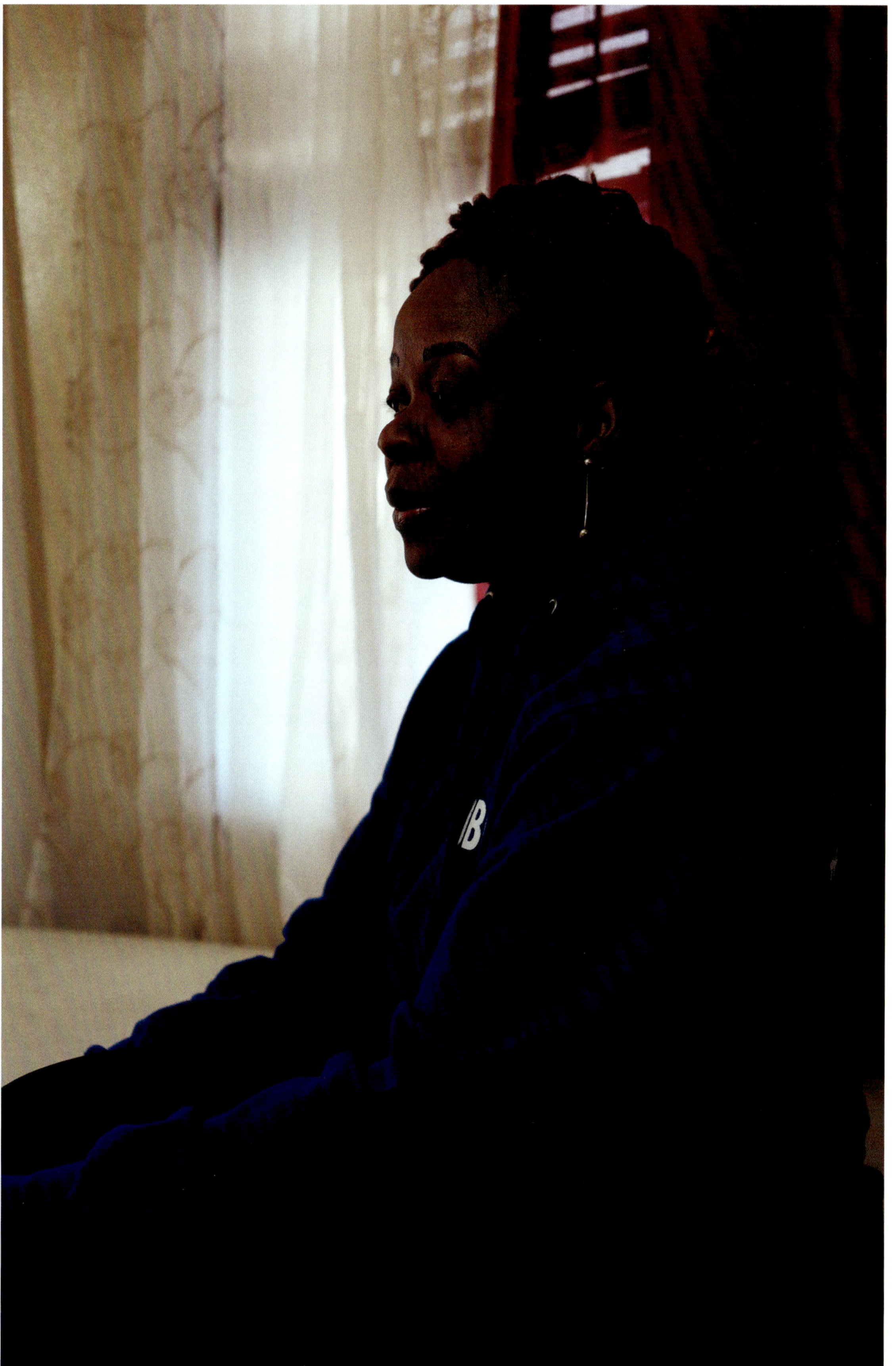

"Growing up, we used to fight every day, twenty-four seven," Shayne recalled on January twenty-eighth. "We were always bumping heads, but all that stopped, and everything was just straight love–everything, everything..."

"He's younger than everybody, so the way he spoke to people–this is my younger brother we're talking about–he used to make me feel like, 'Why didn't I ever think of that?'"

"He was just becoming the man we all wanted him to be."

"There will never be another Tyler on this earth again. It's just the way he was. He was one of a kind. You can't replace him."

"They call it a grieving process, but it's not a process, it's a lifetime."

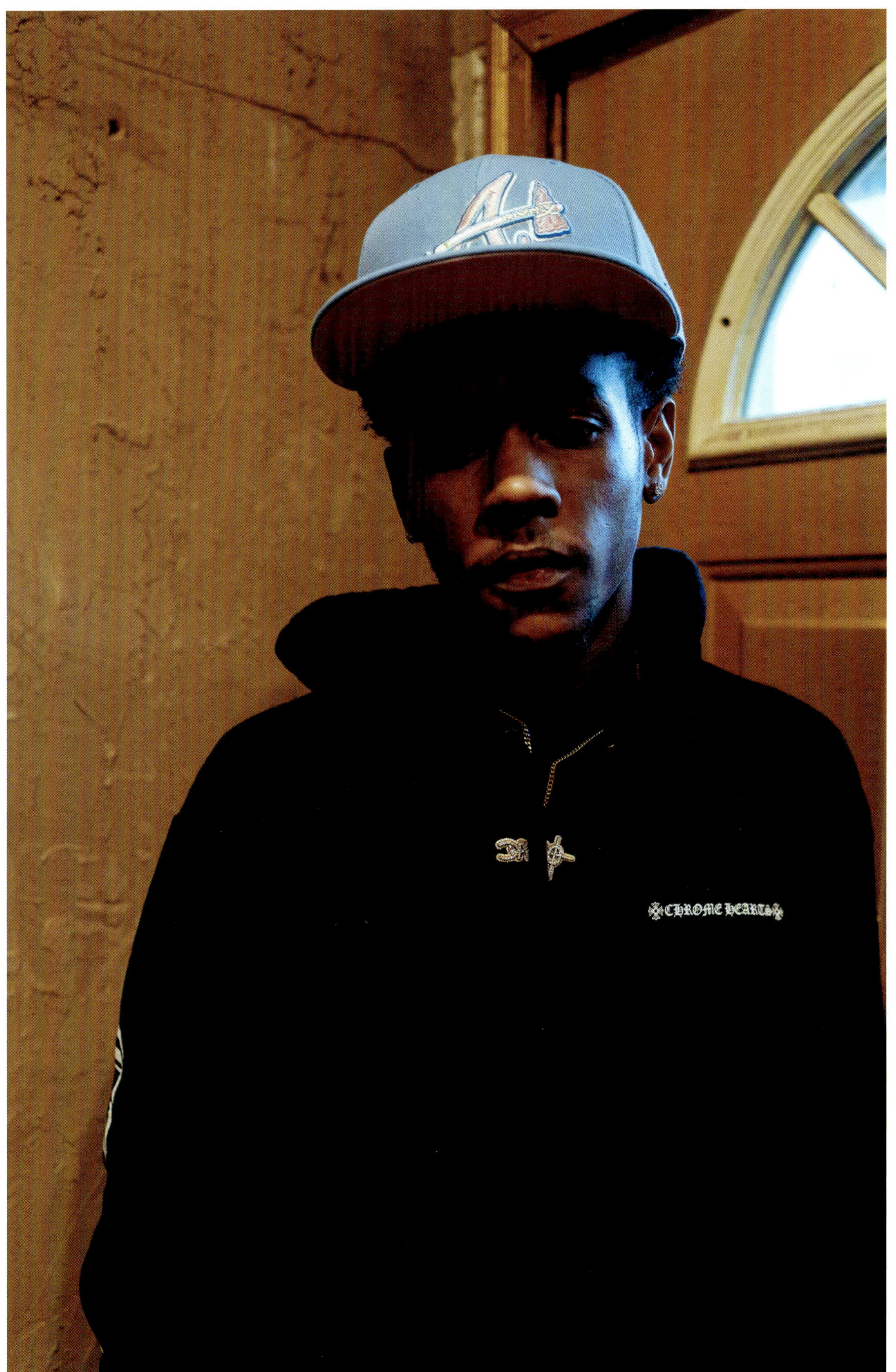
CHROME HEARTS

Shomari Nichols; February 3, 2021.

Remembering his little brother as "a righteous young kid" who developed into "a doer and a peacemaker," Shomari knows that "you don't have to be looking for trouble for trouble to find you," but he also knows that what happened to his brother makes no sense. "And just like that," he said, "life changes."

"It's sad, it's sad what happened to Tyler, but knowing him and how resourceful he was, if there's something you can do from the other side, he'd be trying to do it."

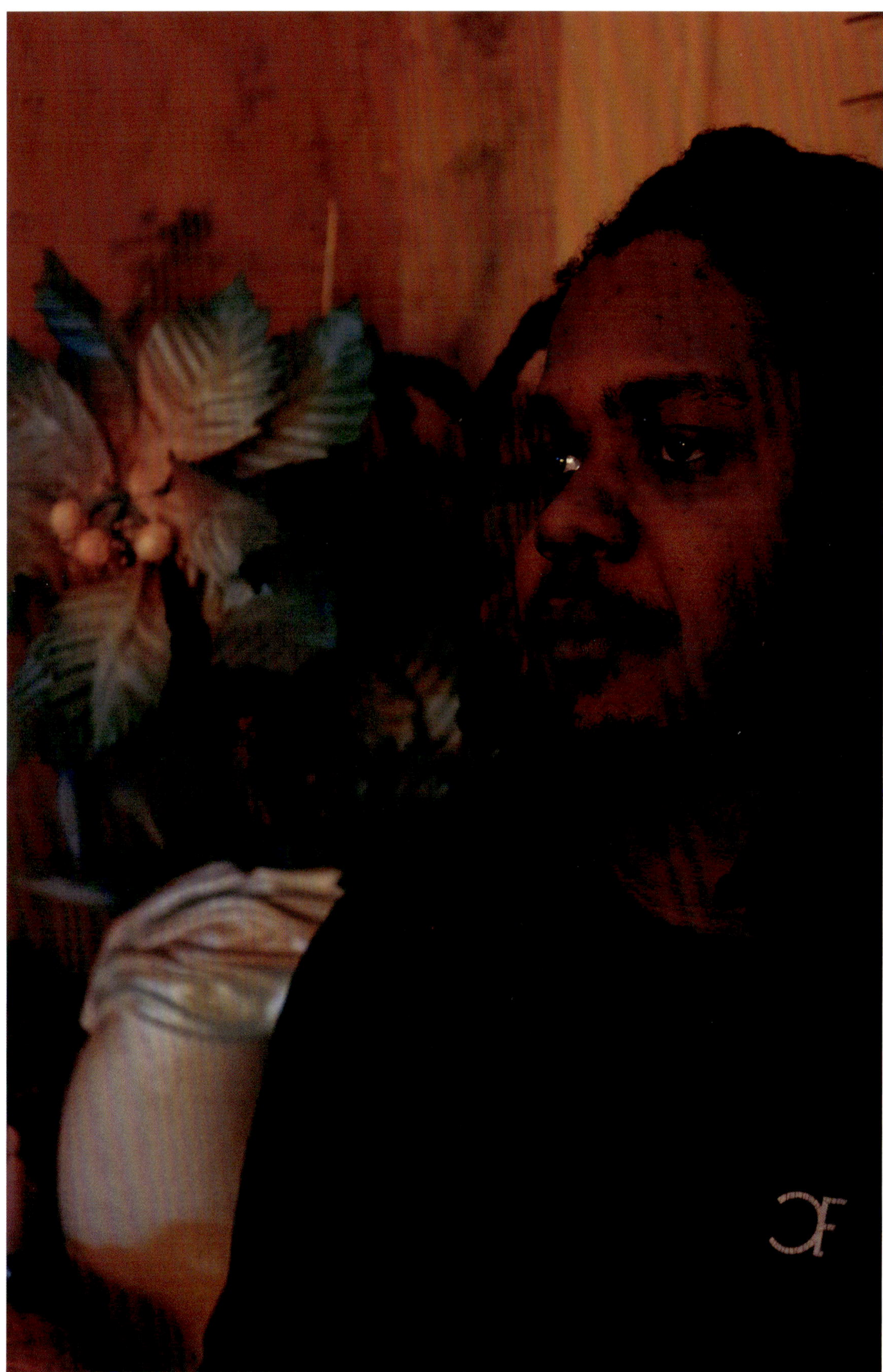

Kareem Eusebe, Tyler's first cousin; February 3, 2021.

"This is our ground. I grew up here, we all grew up here, and we were friends with everyone on the street. It's a diverse culture. We have friends from all different backgrounds and all different ethnicities. Nothing ever happened here.... This is a stain on life."

"Beyond just the loss, nothing is the same."

"This is the hardest hit the family has ever taken."

"This is the hardest moment of my life."

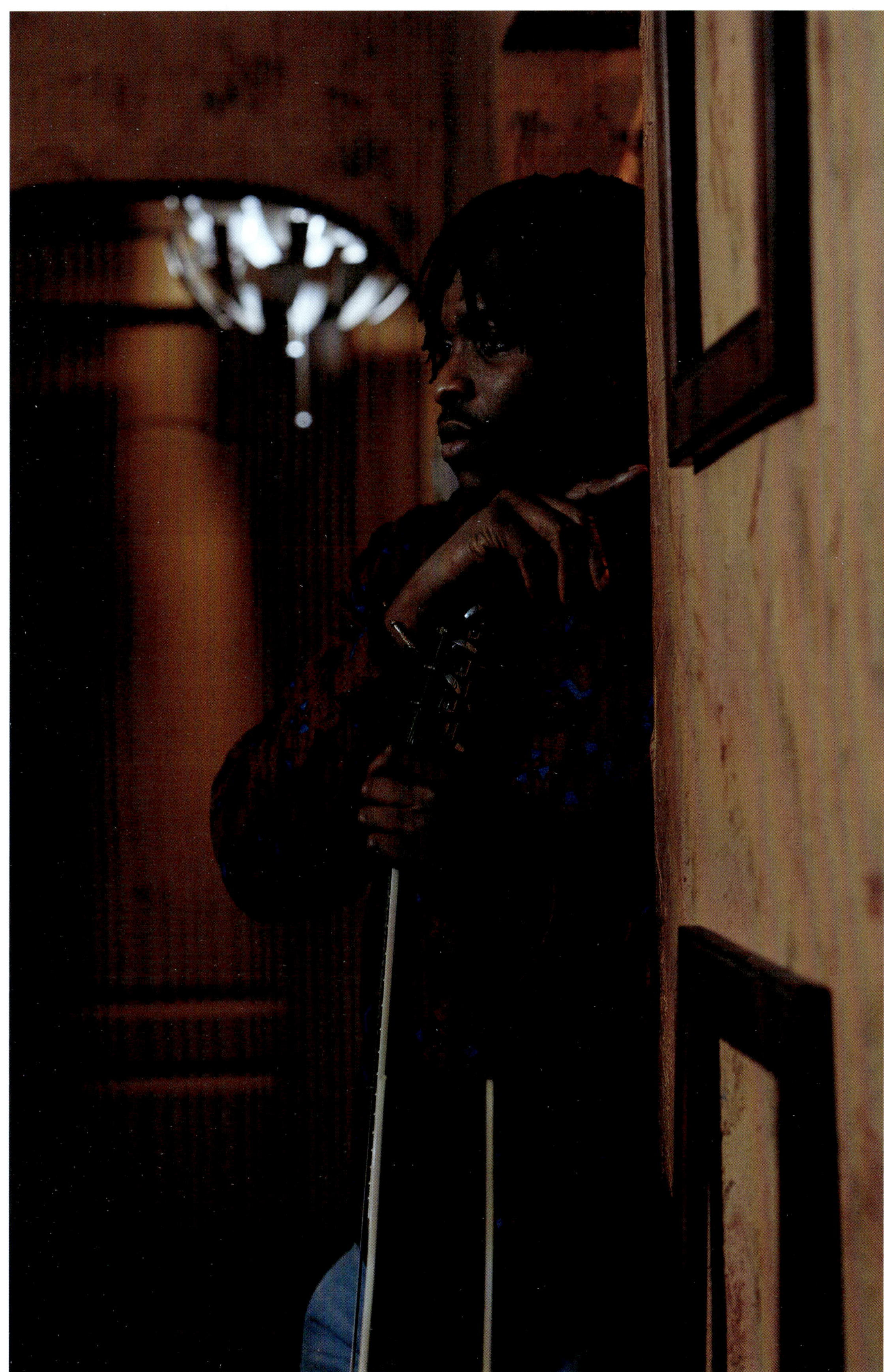

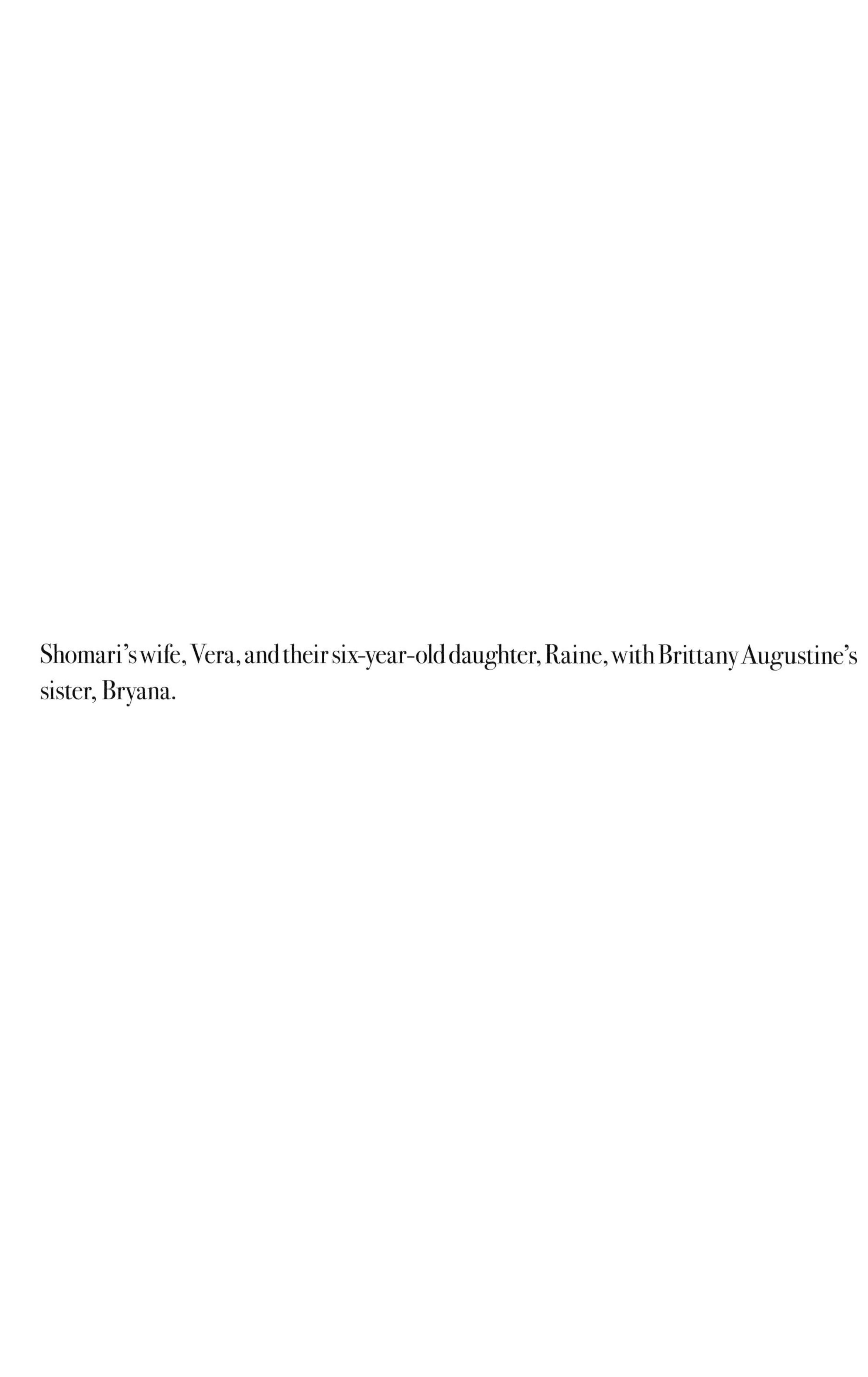

Shomari's wife, Vera, and their six-year-old daughter, Raine, with Brittany Augustine's sister, Bryana.

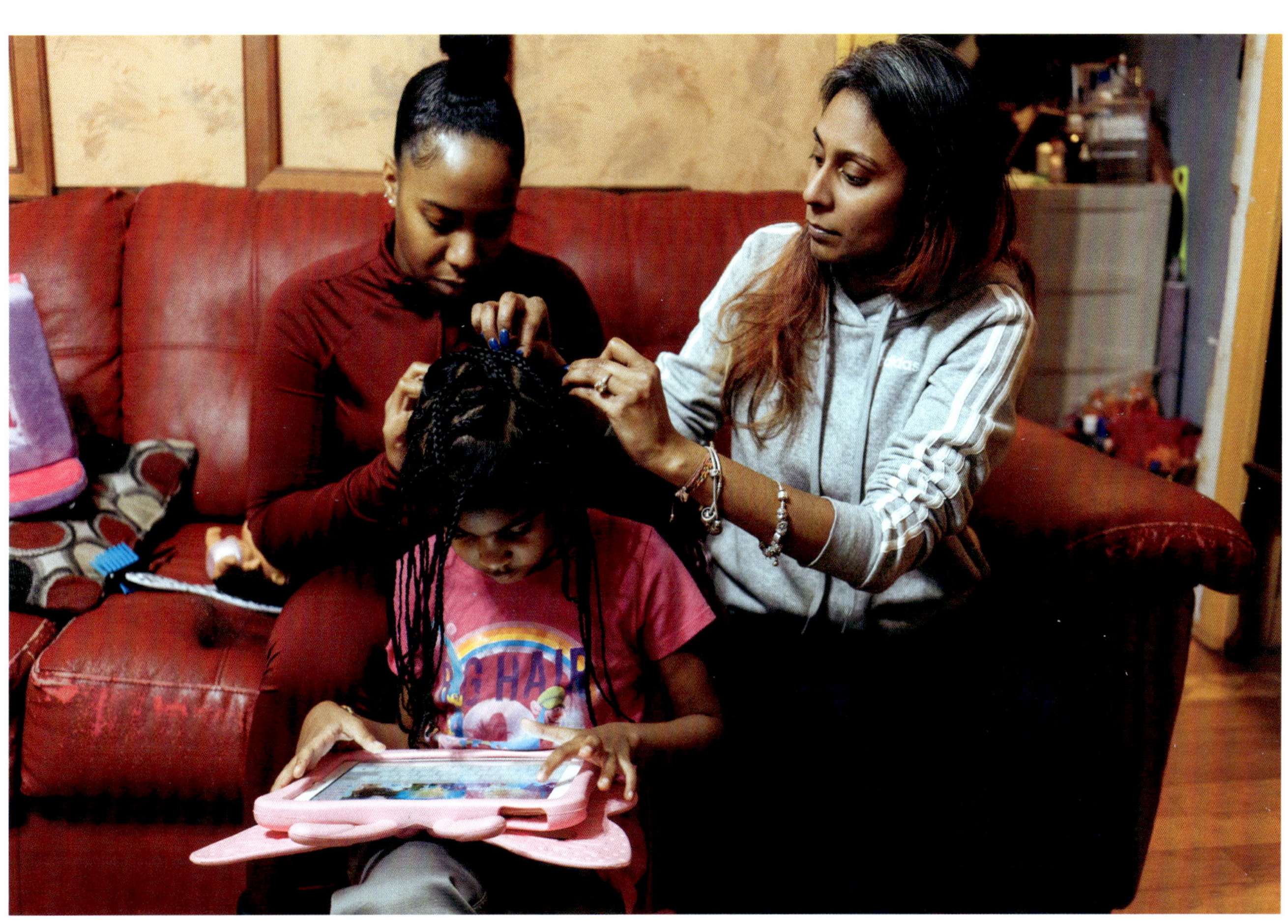

Raine says her bedtime prayers twice every night, once in English and once in Hindi. In the past, the English prayer had always been:

Now I lay me down to sleep
When angels watch us through the night
They keep us in a blessed sight.

After Tyler's death, however, she changed the prayer on her own, dropping the word *angels* and substituting it with the names of departed relatives and friends. The new version goes as follows:

I see Auntie Punky, Uncle Tyler,
Snuggles, Momo, and my other ancestors
Watch us through the night
And keep us in a blessed sight.
Amen.

Auntie Punky was her mother's sister; Momo was a friend of her mother's who committed suicide at sixteen; and Snuggles was Tyler's aged cat.

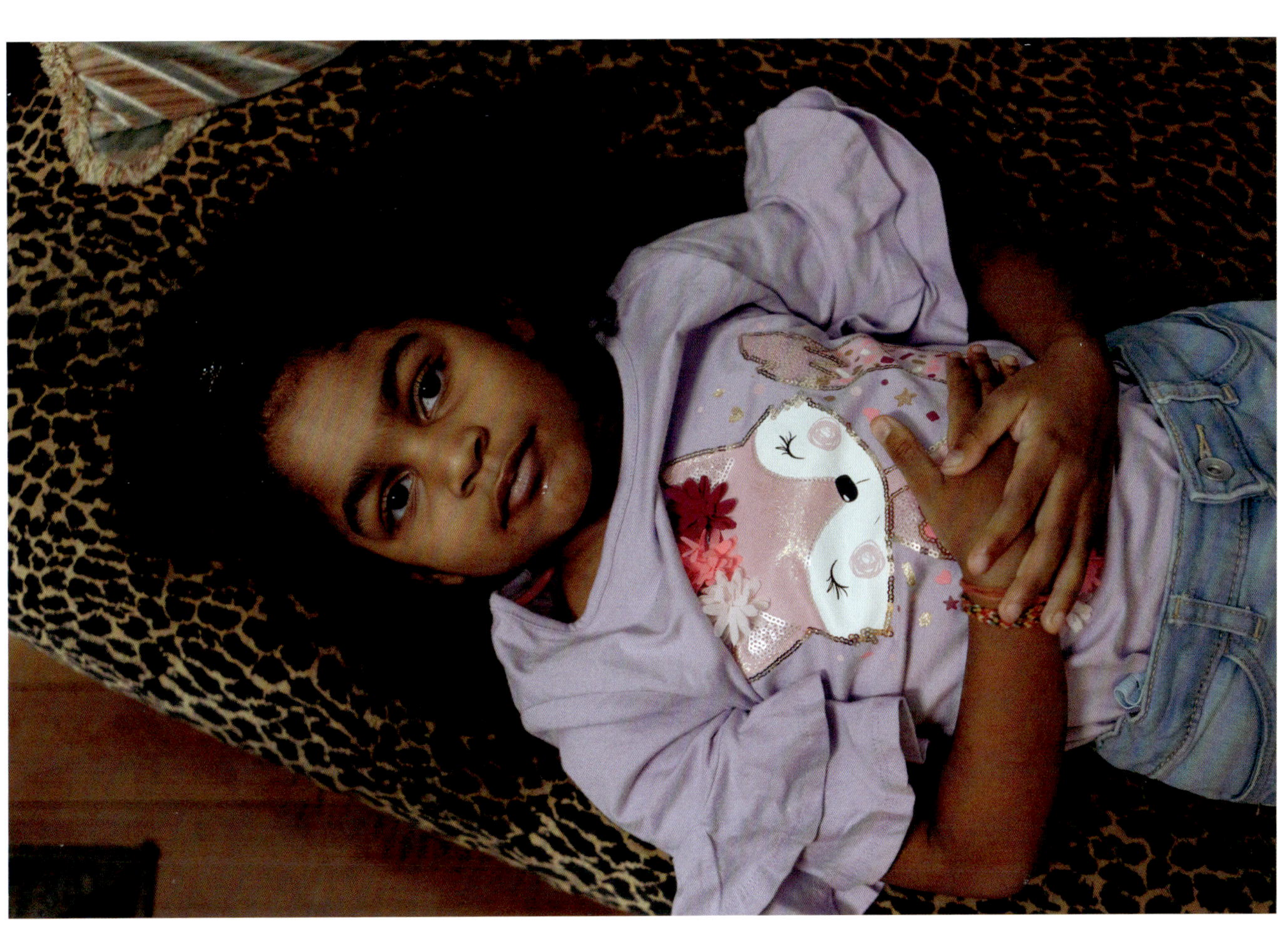

Desirée Chambers, Tyler's aunt; April 3, 2021.

Sherma's younger sister has been an elementary school teacher for the past thirteen years and is the mother of a fourteen-year-old boy and a twelve-year-old girl. Starting when she was in her late teens herself, she often took care of the Nichols boys when their mother was off at work and grew extremely close to them. Among her strongest memories from those early years are countless excursions to the park, braiding the kids' hair, and the pleasure she took in giving them presents. When Tyler was little, she recalls, "he was mature and wise for his age, but still playful. He would punch me all the time—until my arm hurt—and squeeze me, squeeze me so tight. I couldn't attack him head-on [because he was too fast]. I had to sneak up on him."

As the years went by, he became "a very calm spirit." What impressed her most was how rational he was, continually thinking about "how things should be" and asking questions about right and wrong and the proper way to live. "That's something I'm really proud of," she said, "and that's why we tried so hard to get him into college." The problem was that his mother couldn't afford the tuition and yet earned too much for him to qualify as a candidate for a substantial scholarship. The only solution would have been a student loan, but Sherma didn't want her son to start out in life saddled with debt, so a compromise was struck, and Tyler wound up going to trade school instead. It's not that he was unhappy with the alternative, his aunt said, but even though she was proud of him for doing well at his studies, she is tormented by a feeling that she "failed him," and now that Tyler is dead, she can't help wondering if he wouldn't still be alive today if he had gone to college after all. "I keep going back and thinking how I could have changed the trajectory of what happened to him. Really, it's hard."

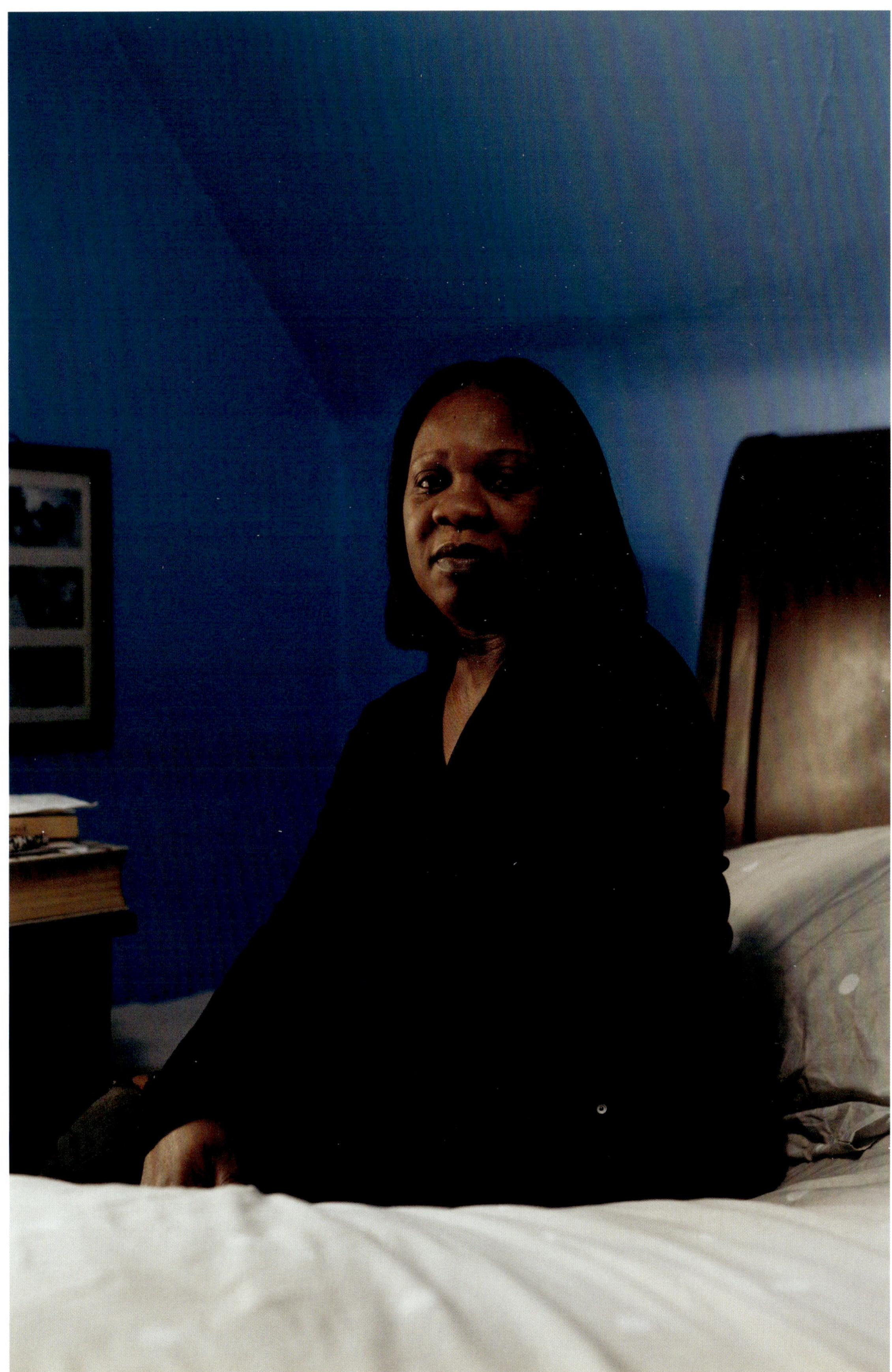

When asked how she had been holding up since December, she said: "I have good days and I have bad. Just yesterday, I was sitting at my Mom's [on the third floor of the house], and he crossed my mind, and I teared up and started to cry. It's difficult . . . knowing that he's not here anymore. You operate like a zombie. I know there are things I have to do. I have to go to work, I have to get up, I have to take care of my kids, but I'm not doing it with a full heart, I'm just going though the motions."

Since Tyler's death, she has helped out Sherma on numerous practical fronts, among them applying for a grant from the Office of Victim Services to cover the costs of the funeral. "I'm putting down the deceased's name, Tyler Nichols, and it's so hard because it's real....I have his death certificate over there, buried under a pile of papers. Everything has to be buried, because I can't think about him not being here" *(starts to cry).*

"Why did it have to happen to us? Kareem would say that we didn't need this kind of lesson. You go through life and you try to be kind and you try to be helpful and you try to be supportive even to strangers, anybody you can support and help, and we just feel we're being punished because he's been taken from us..."

On responding to the news that the police have estimated it will take at least two years before the person they have arrested is put on trial: "I thought I would feel better after they caught someone, but I don't feel any better. There's still an open wound, and I think about having to wait so long to see this person and hoping he's convicted for the crime he committed...We're never going to forget Tyler, but I'm assuming that in the next two or three years it's not going to be as painful as it is right now, and I'm afraid that when the trial comes it's going to open up that wound and make us feel we're back to the day it happened, the week it happened, two weeks after it happened. That's what I'm afraid of. I'm not looking forward to it."

On her fourteen-year-old son, who looked up to his Uncle Tyler and greatly admired him: "He's angry. He doesn't want to think about what happened, because it just makes him angry. You never know what's going to happen. You try to be as safe as possible, so I let him go out, but nervously. I have to let him go out. I can't keep him a prisoner."

Carlene Chambers, Tyler's aunt; April 30, 2021. Sherma's older sister and the mother of two of Tyler's cousin's, Kareem and Latoya. She has been employed as a registered nurse by Coney Island Hospital for more than twenty years.

"I watched him from birth to the last day of his life."

"When he died, a part of me went with him."

"I don't think we'll ever get over it—not ever."

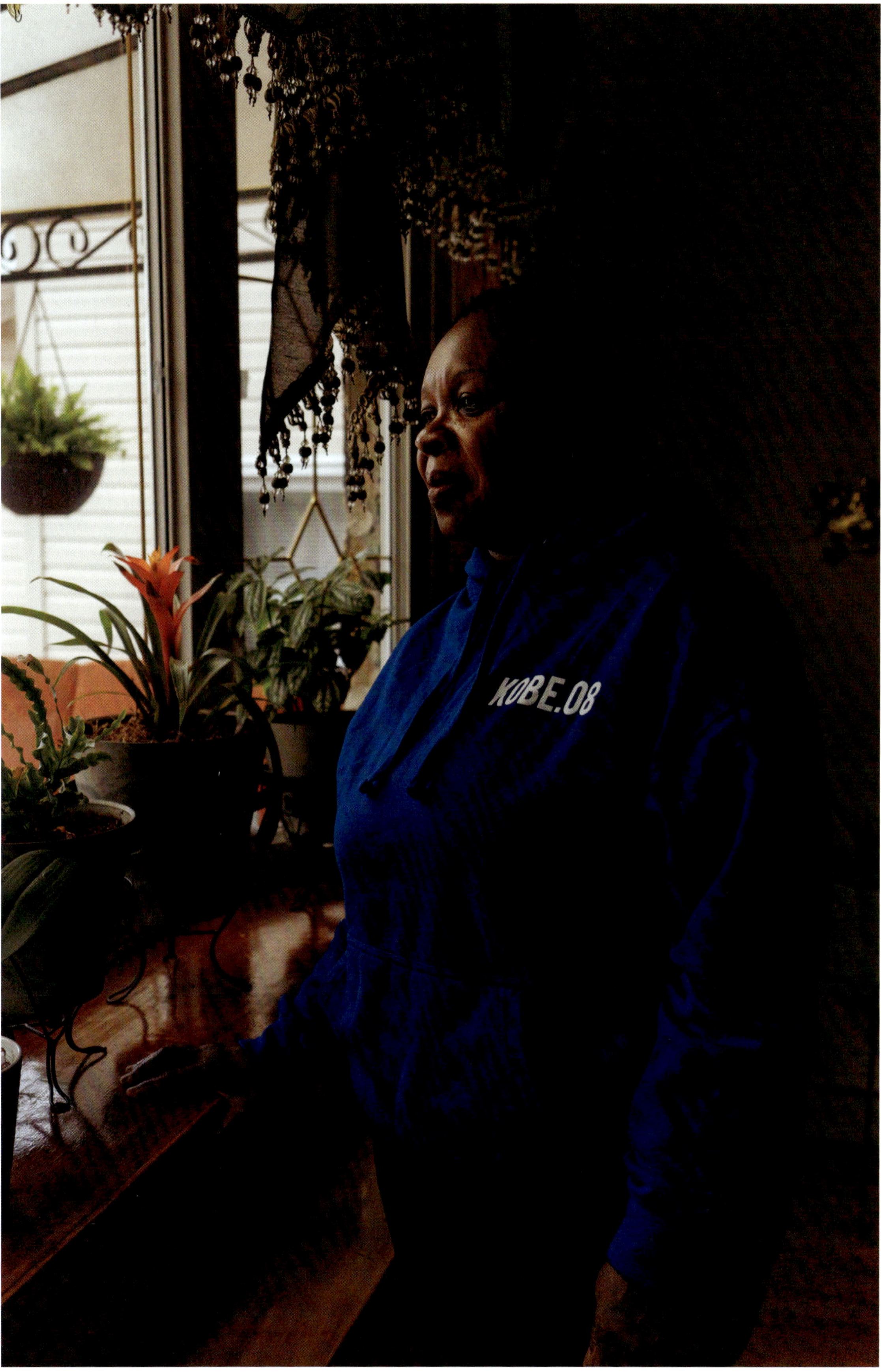
KOBE.08

Elizabeth Chambers, Tyler's grandmother; May 2, 2021.

"I'm seventy-nine years old, and this is the hardest thing I've ever been through."

"I keep telling Shayne and Shomari and Kareem that we just have to live through this. But we'll never get over it."

"They took something that was so dear to us..."

"They say that time heals all wounds–but no, I don't think so."

"We've always been a close-knit family, but Tyler's death has brought us even closer."

"Poor Ashley."

"Poor Kareem–he's just so torn."

"I keep looking out the window into the backyard, and I see Tyler down there walking the dog."

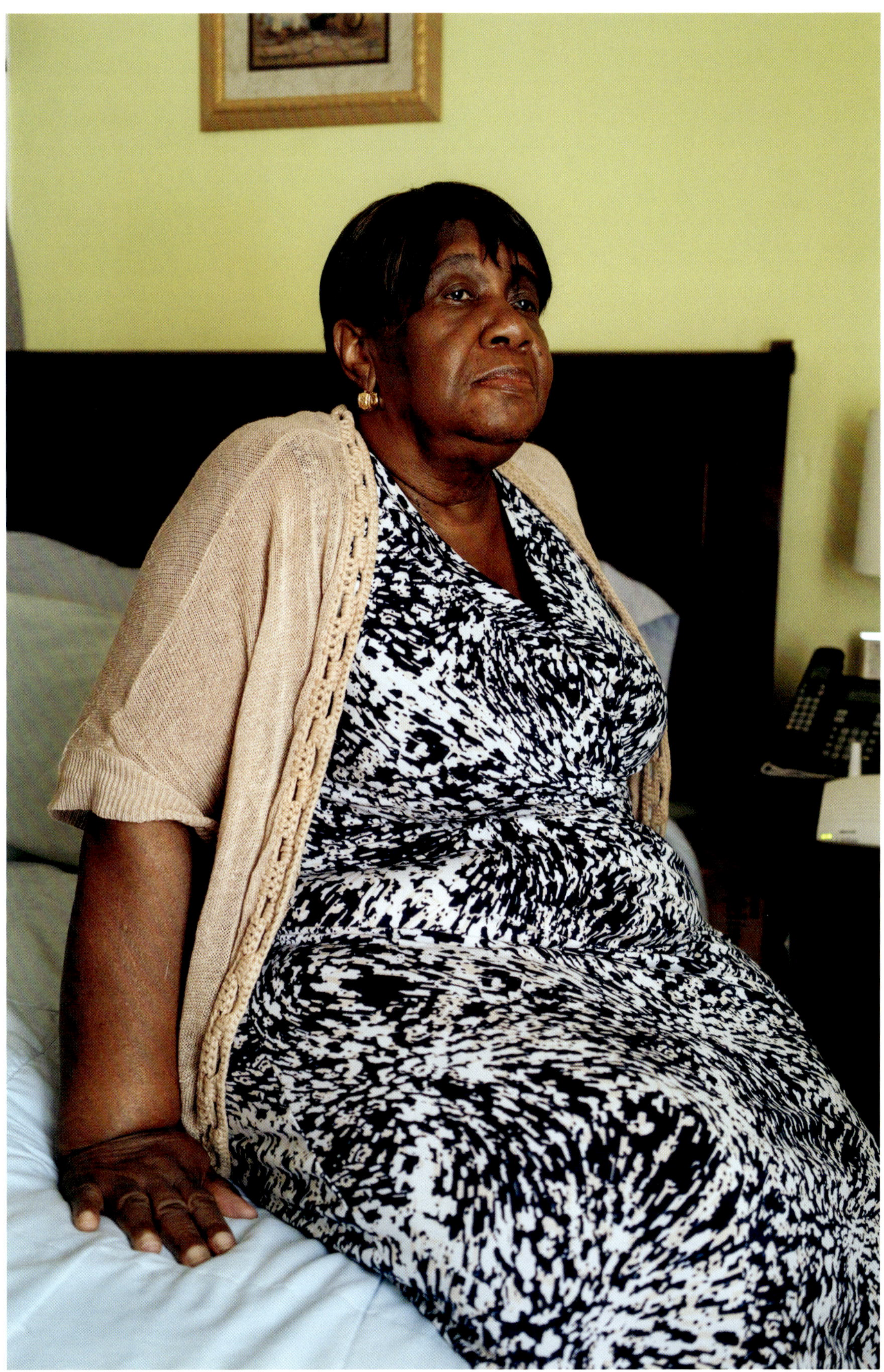

Garnet Nichols, Tyler's father; April 30, 2021.

The fifty-nine-year-old Garnet Nichols was born in Saint Vincent and moved to Brooklyn when he was seventeen. After graduating from the Apex Technical School as an HVAC specialist (heating and air conditioning), he has been steadily employed by the Downstate Medical Center for the past thirty-one years and supplements his income by buying and trading stocks. He was classified as an essential worker during the Covid-19 pandemic and, in addition to his regular work in the permanent buildings of the facility, was responsible for temperature control in the numerous auxiliary tents that were put up to accommodate the vast influx of Covid-19 patients, many of whom died, as did several of his coworkers and various members of the staff.

He and Sherma were married in 1995 and divorced in 2012. He now lives in another part of Brooklyn, but he and Sherma have not broken off contact, and he is still looked upon as a member of the family. Just as important, he has never distanced himself from his sons and continues to be involved with them, as well as with his young granddaughter, Raine. By way of example, he mentioned that in recent years he has been using portions of his extra money to set up bank accounts in trust for his boys—without telling them—and that the last one he opened, on December 23, 2020, was for Tyler—which happened to be the day Tyler was killed.

After his son's death, he took a month off from work, but the horror has not diminished in the months since then, and he lives in a state of continual despondency, immobilized by grief. Most of his spare time is now spent in a basement room of his house, where he sifts through and studies early photographs of Tyler and his brothers and cries, he said, "cries every day."

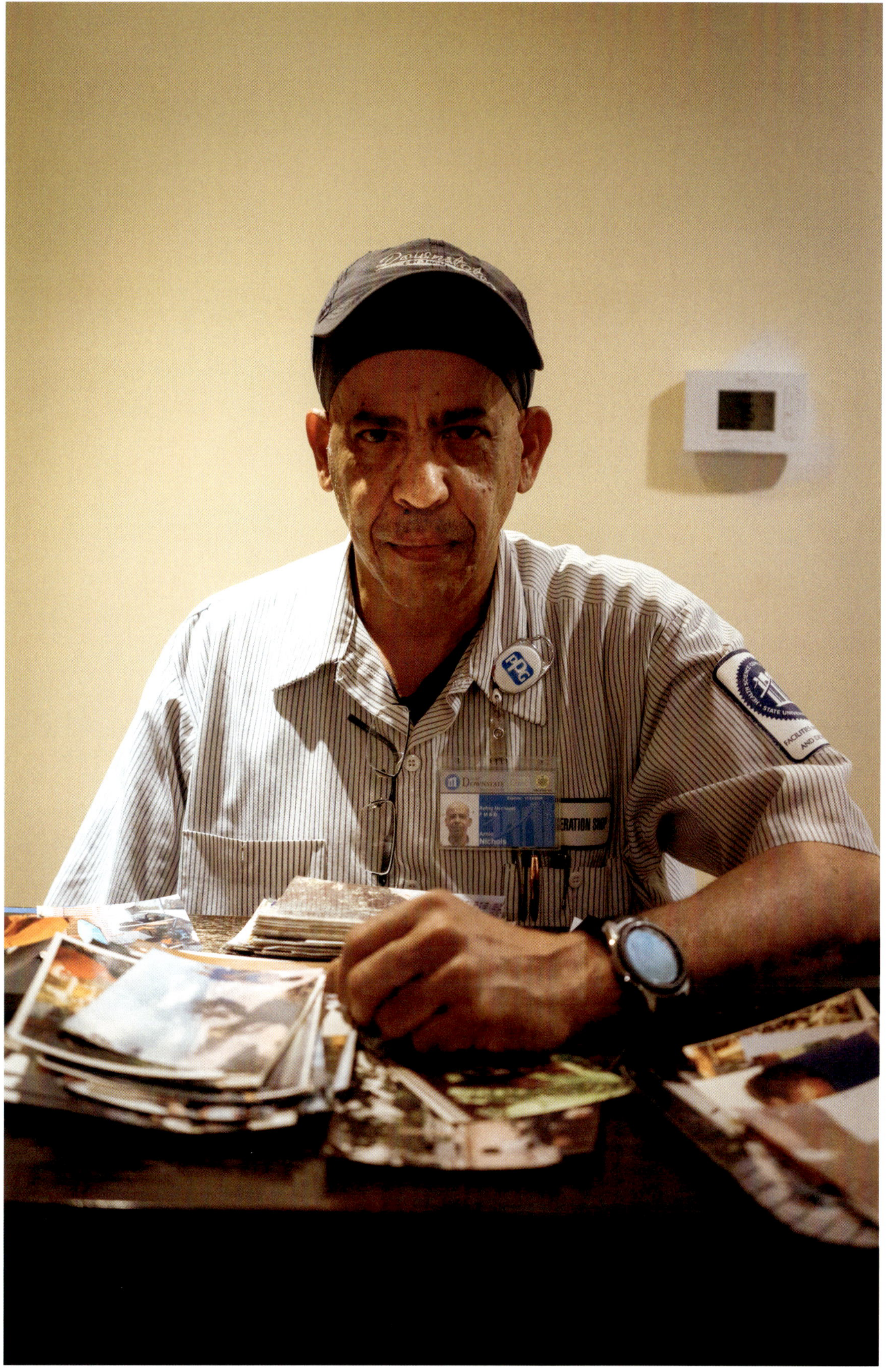
PPG
DOWNSTATE
Nichols
ERATION SHOP

Garnet Nichols, Jr., Tyler's brother; May 2, 2021.

Known to everyone in the family as Junior, Garnet Nichols's oldest son is the product of an earlier marriage that ended in divorce. The boy grew up in Brooklyn, for the most part with his mother, but weekends were spent at the Chambers-Nichols house in Kensington, where he became close to his stepmother, Sherma, and his three half-brothers, especially the smallest and youngest one, Tyler. After graduating from high school, he left the United States and lived in Saint Vincent for the next ten years, all the while maintaining contact with his brothers through occasional visits and frequent Facebook exchanges. After returning to Brooklyn in 2016, he quickly reintegrated himself into the family circle, again gravitating toward Tyler as the brother he felt he had "the most in common with," as he explained during a talk at the apartment he shares with his girlfriend. On the night of December twenty-third, he came running to the house the instant Shomari texted him that Tyler had been stabbed.

On the family house and neighborhood: "It was always like paradise to me, a sweet place. Indians, Russians, all kinds of different people, all of them minding their own business. Then something like this happens, and it makes you question everything."

Pointing to the gash in the wall behind him: "I punched this in. I woke up one morning, and I just felt mad. So I bashed in the wall–boom–and then I asked myself why the hell would you do that, messing up your own place? But you get so frustrated, you just can't stop yourself..."

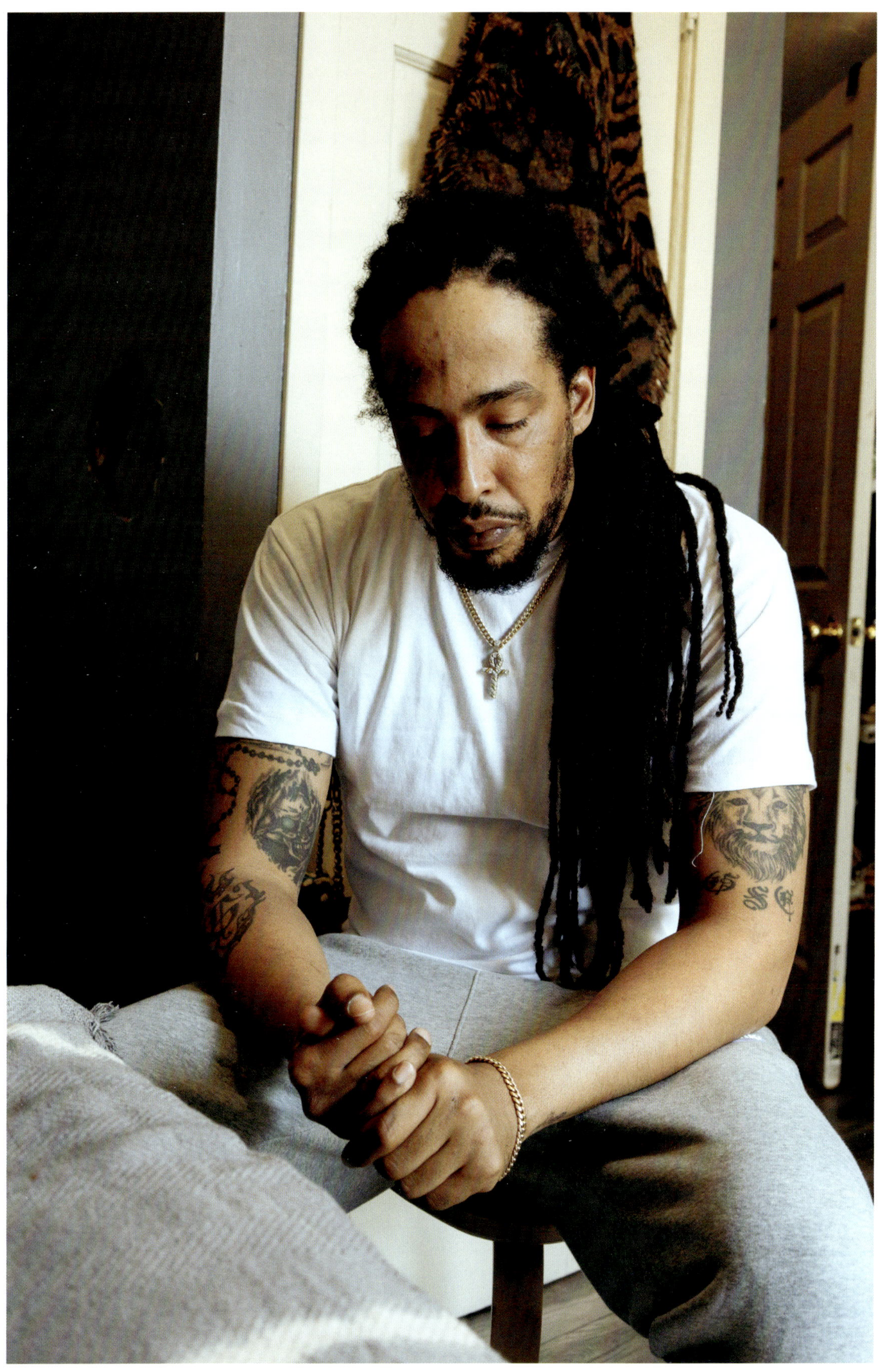

Candles lit for Tyler during one of the forty days after his death. As Sherma explained to Ostrander, the forty-day ritual is widely practiced throughout the Caribbean and is "a way to put the dead person's soul at rest. Everyone in the family lights a candle, and they can say whatever they feel to him. It's to let him know that we're good–and to help him transition."

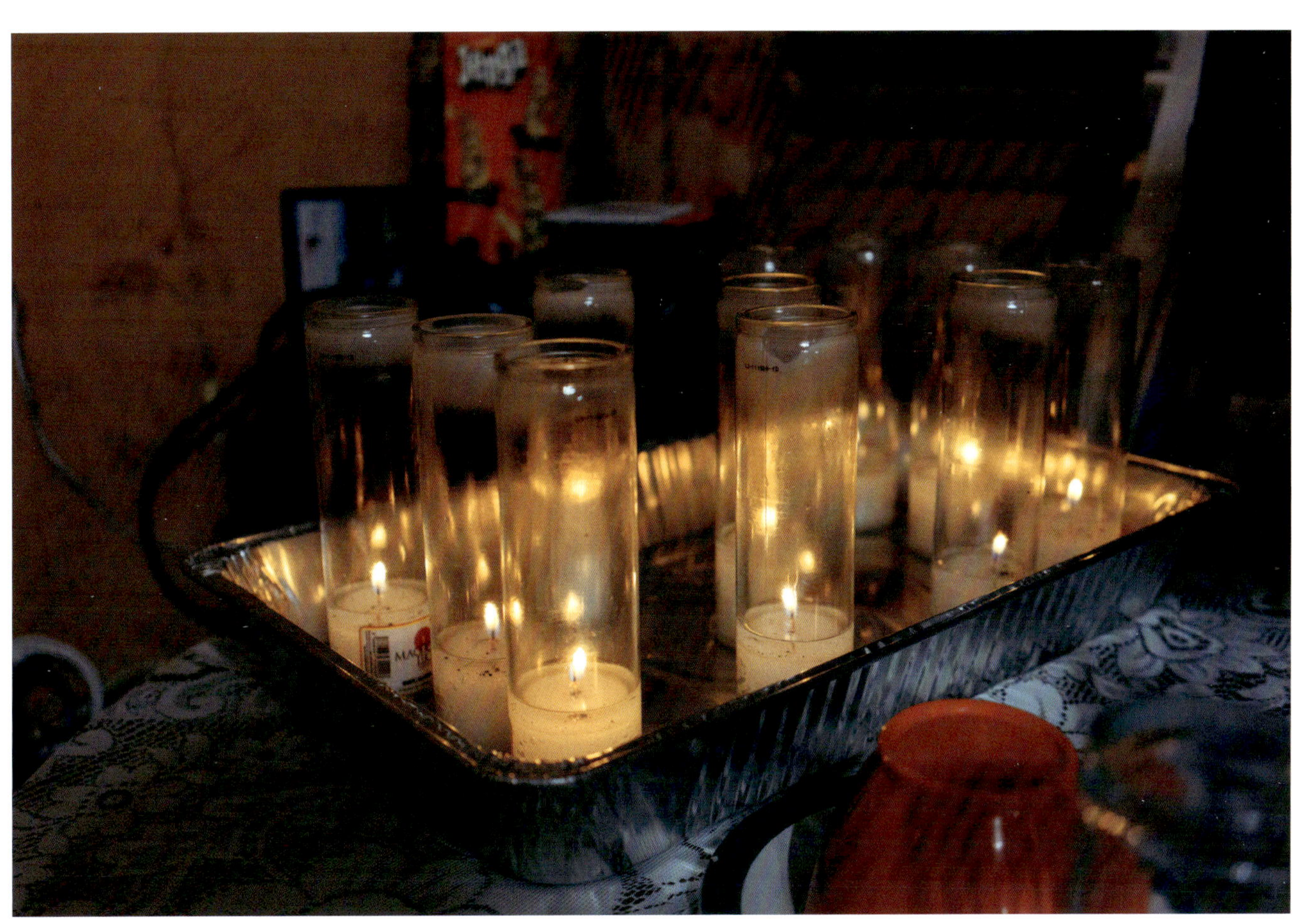

Ashley Duverneau, Tyler's girlfriend; April 3, 2021.

Ashley in the bedroom she shared with Tyler. The pendant hanging from her necklace contains a photograph of them on the evening of their senior prom. It was given to her as a present by the mother of her friend Josh Robles on the day of Tyler's funeral.

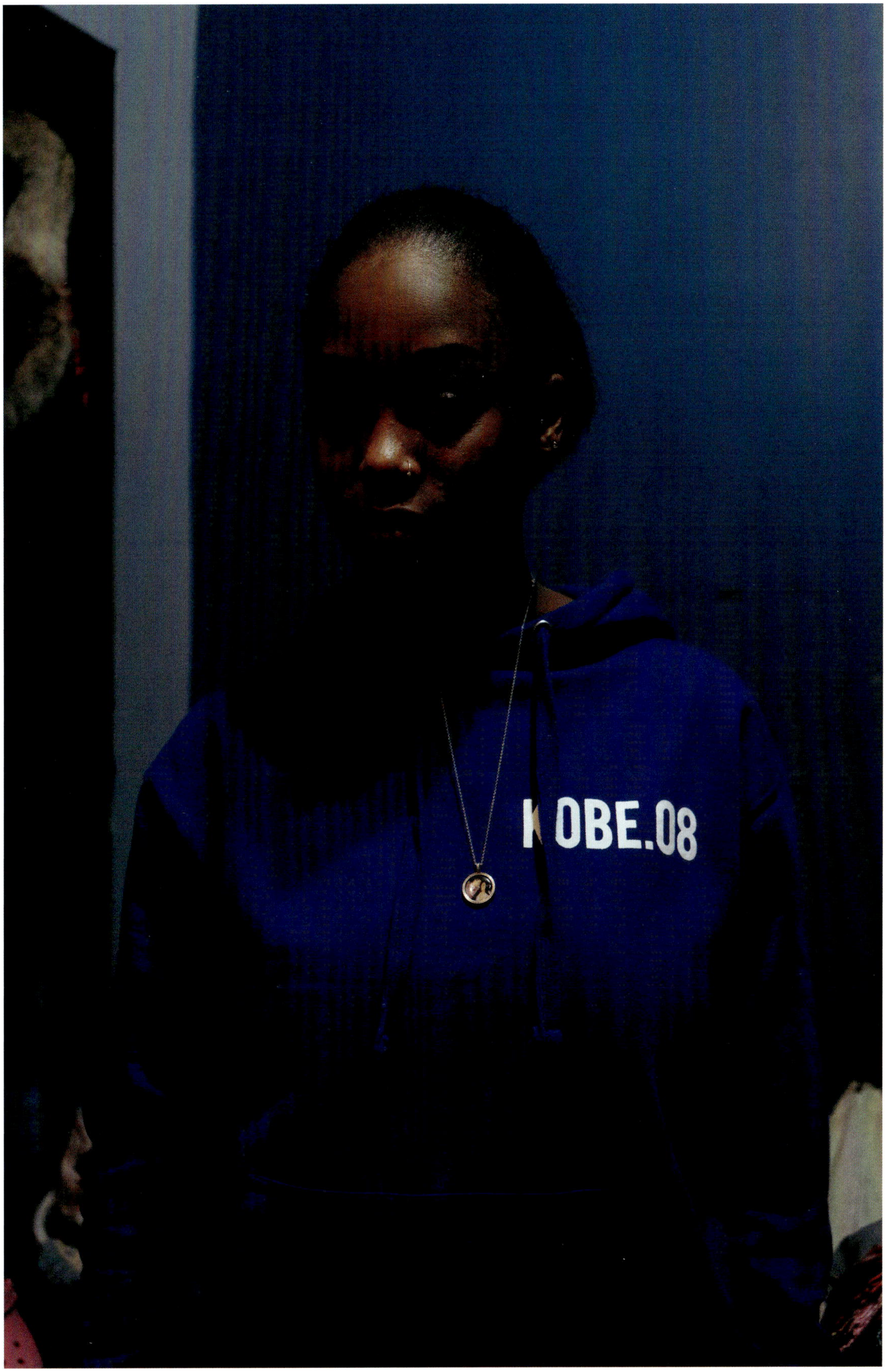

The nightstand in Ashley's bedroom with a Bible open to Psalm 91 and various pieces of jewelry commemorating Tyler. The braid in the plastic bag was Tyler's, which was clipped off by the mortician at the funeral home and given to Ashley. In a conversation on April 23, 2021, Ashley explained that the ninety-first psalm is "a protection psalm" and that "anything negative can happen to you, but nothing can touch you once you are by God." As the tenth and eleventh verses put it:

> *There shall no evil befall thee, neither shall a plague come nigh thy dwelling.*
> *For he shall give his angels charge over thee, to keep thee in all thy ways.*

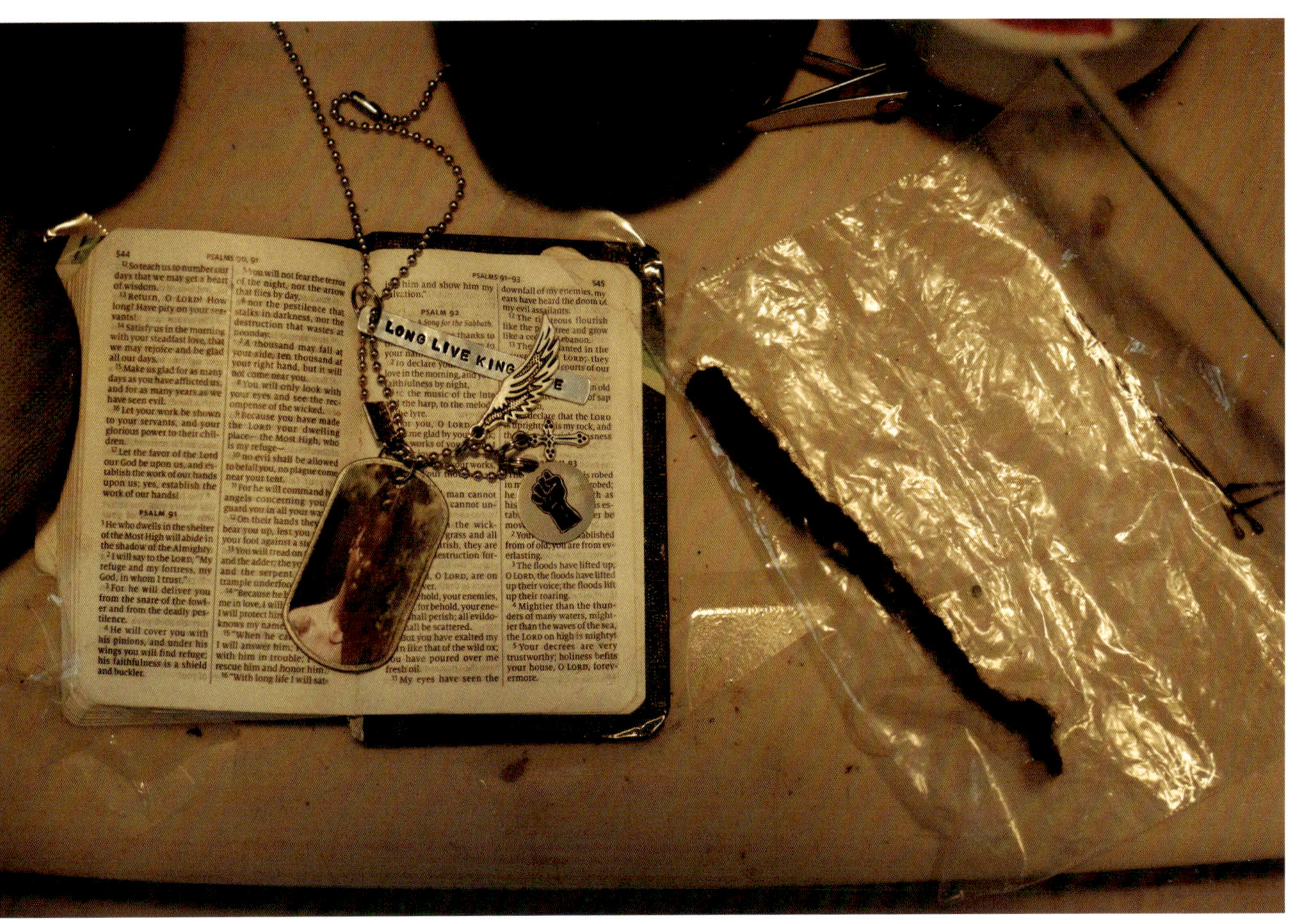

PSALM 91
PSALM 92
LONG LIVE KING

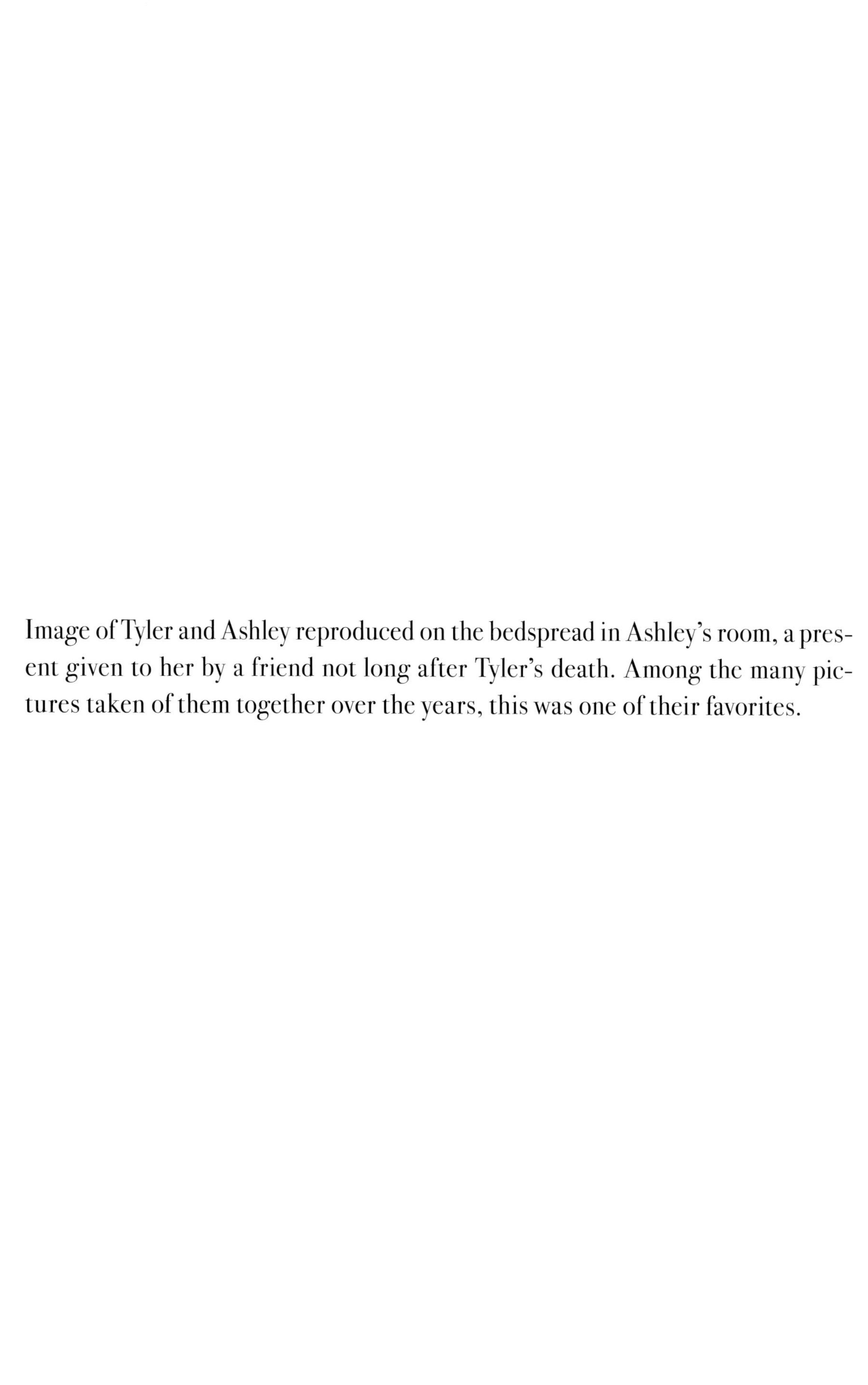

Image of Tyler and Ashley reproduced on the bedspread in Ashley's room, a present given to her by a friend not long after Tyler's death. Among the many pictures taken of them together over the years, this was one of their favorites.

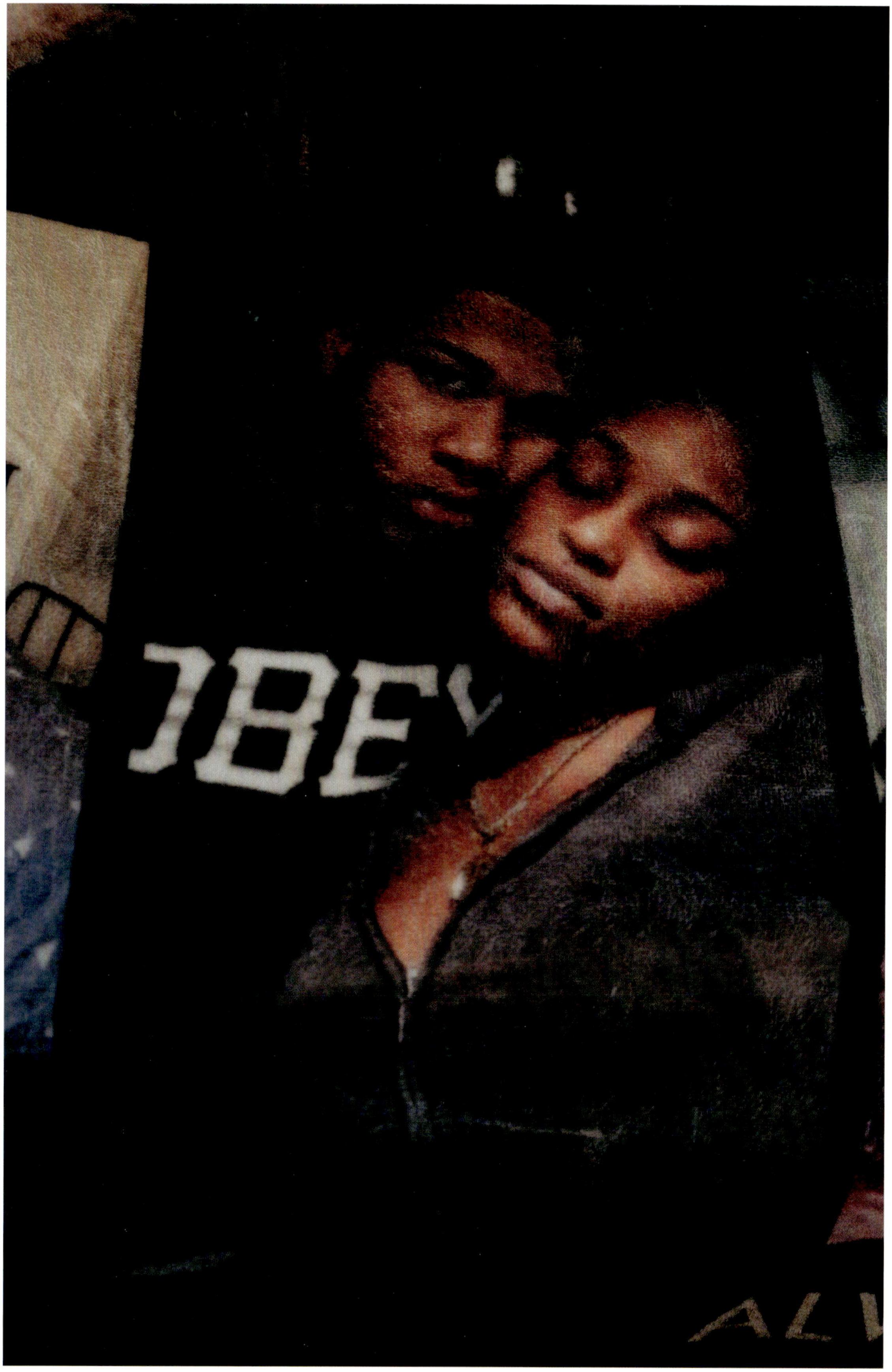

Ashley in the bedroom she shared with Tyler until the night of his murder. Photograph taken on January 28, 2021, one month and five days after.

From the morning of their first encounter as eleven-year-old sixth graders, the longest period of time Ashley and Tyler ever spent apart was twenty days.

Summing up her relationship with Tyler during the three years they lived together in the house, Ashley said that he was continually surprising her with gifts and that "he spoiled me rotten."

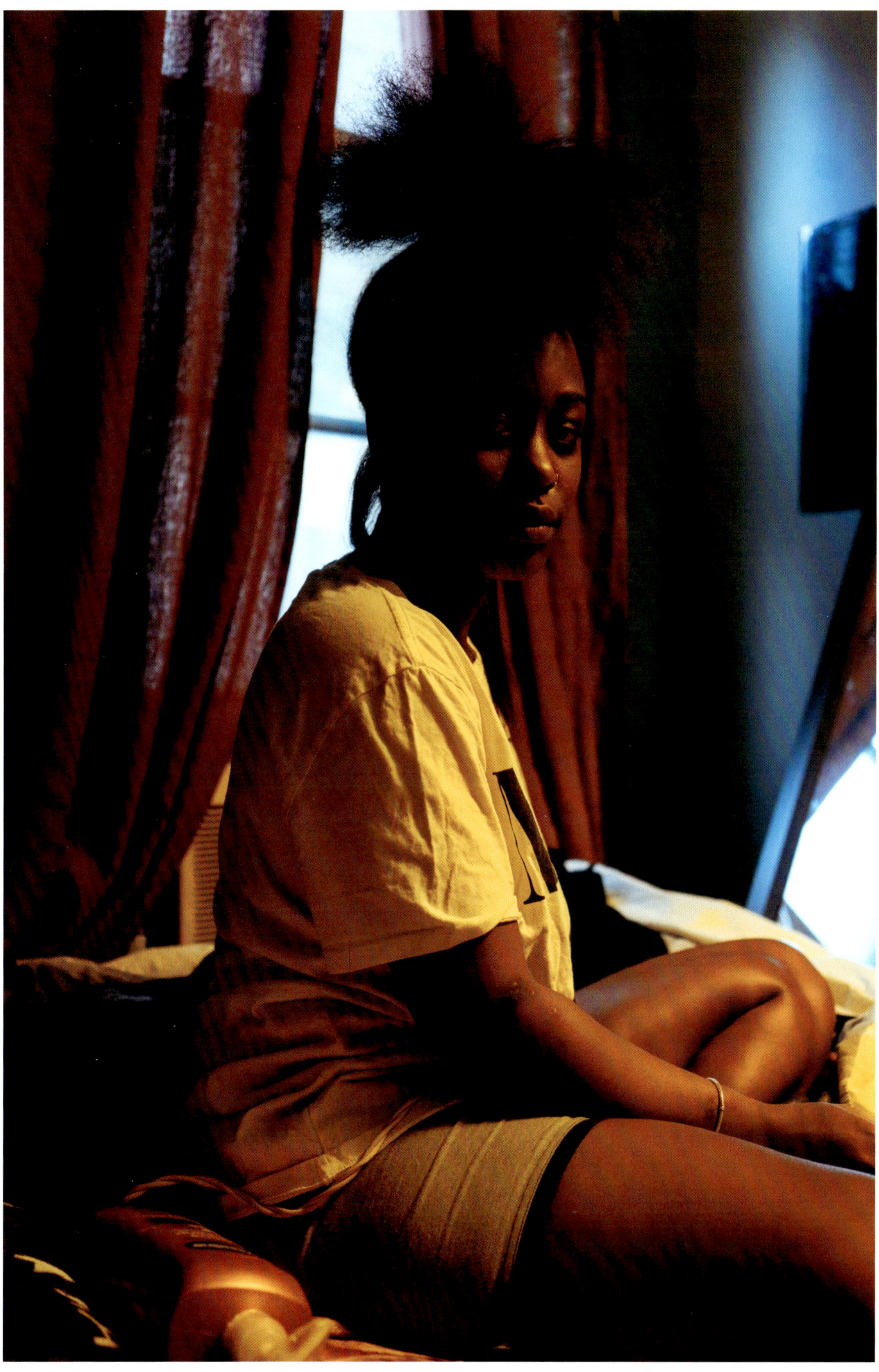

Ashley's shrine on the dressing table in her room. The boots flanking the photograph of Tyler are the ones he was wearing on the night he was killed.

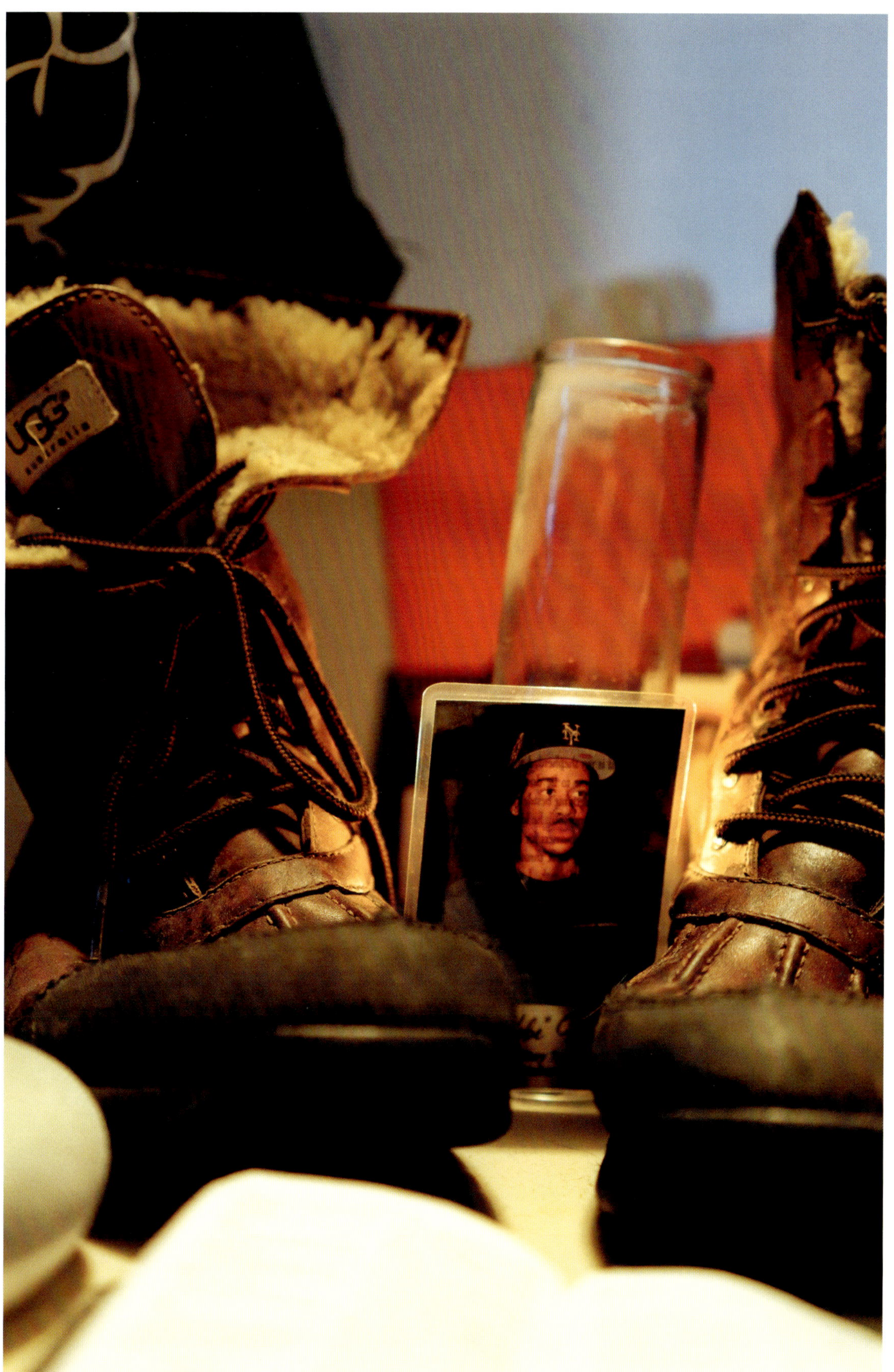
UGG

Brittany Augustine, Shayne's girlfriend and a member of the household; April 3, 2021.

During a conversation on April 23, she struggled to keep her composure as she remarked that "Tyler was like my brother" and remembered how often they had laughed together, and then, after saying that no one could be around him without feeling happy, she broke down and started to cry. After a long pause, she finally managed to say "I'm sorry," and the tape recorder was turned off.

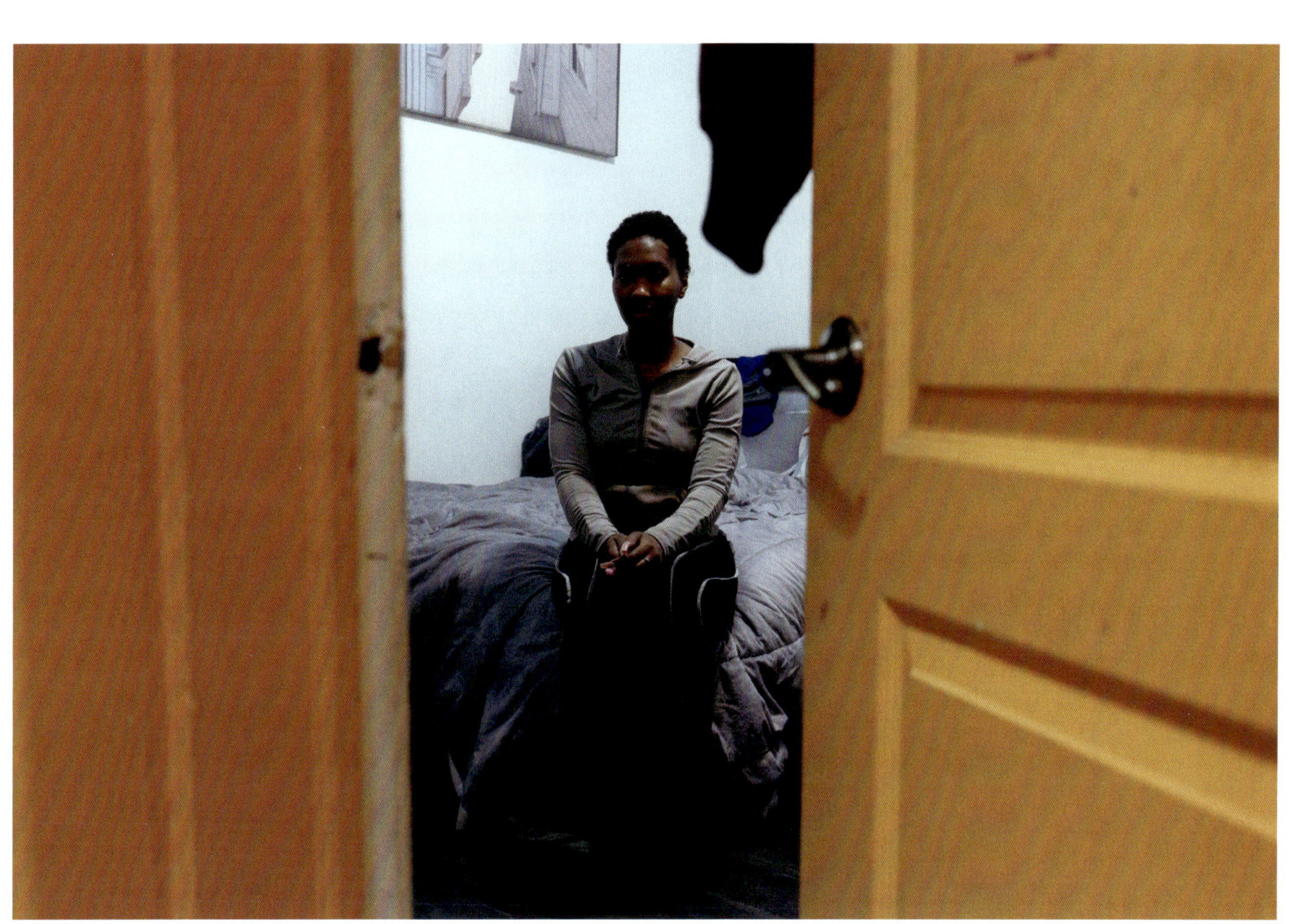

Kessler Jean-Claude, professional rapper and close friend of Tyler's since childhood, displaying memorial tattoo in honor of his friend; April 3, 2021.

"I can't stop thinking about it, and it don't make sense. How everything went down and all that. Tyler was like my brother, basically. Not even like my brother—he *was* my brother."

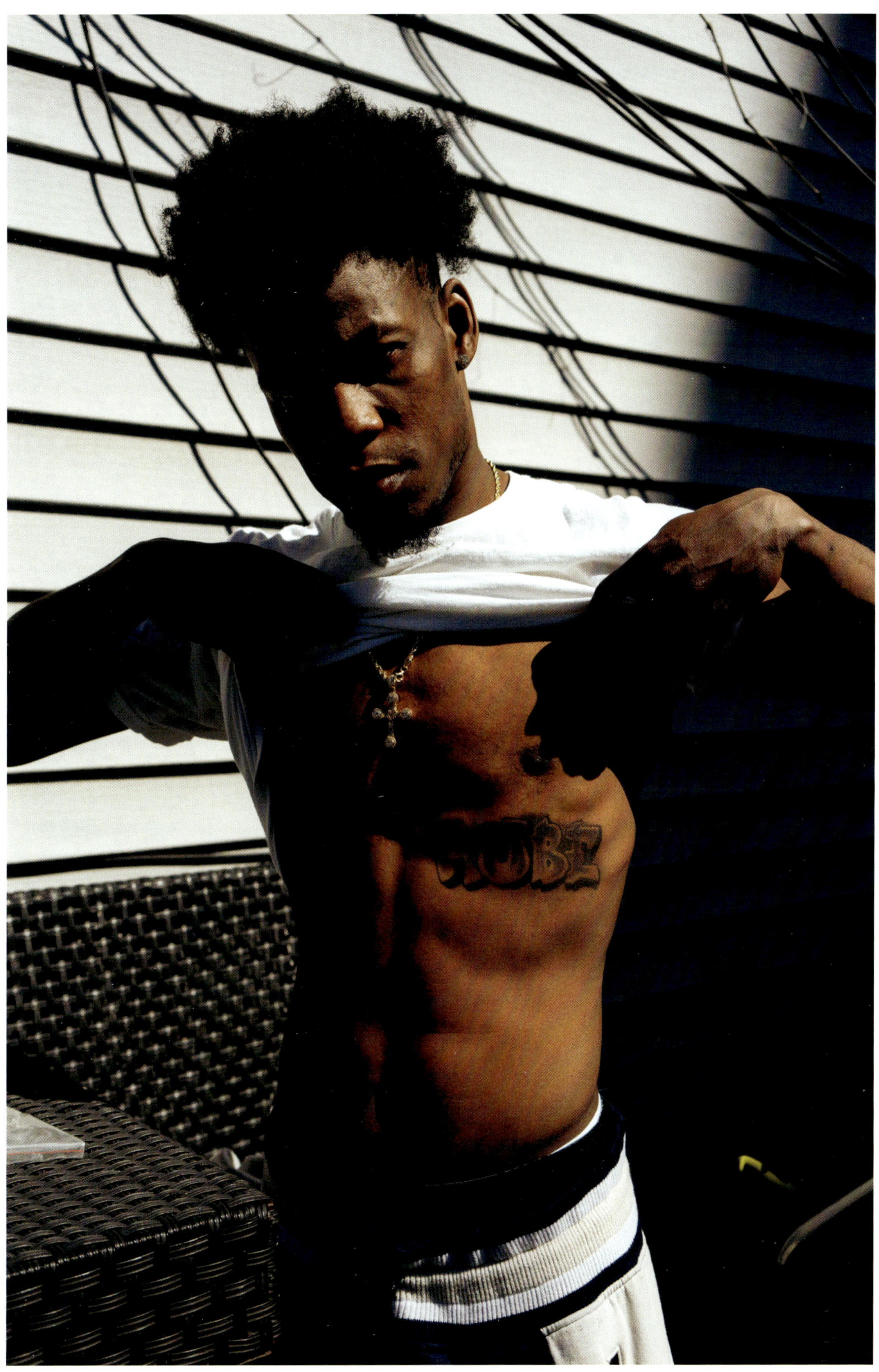

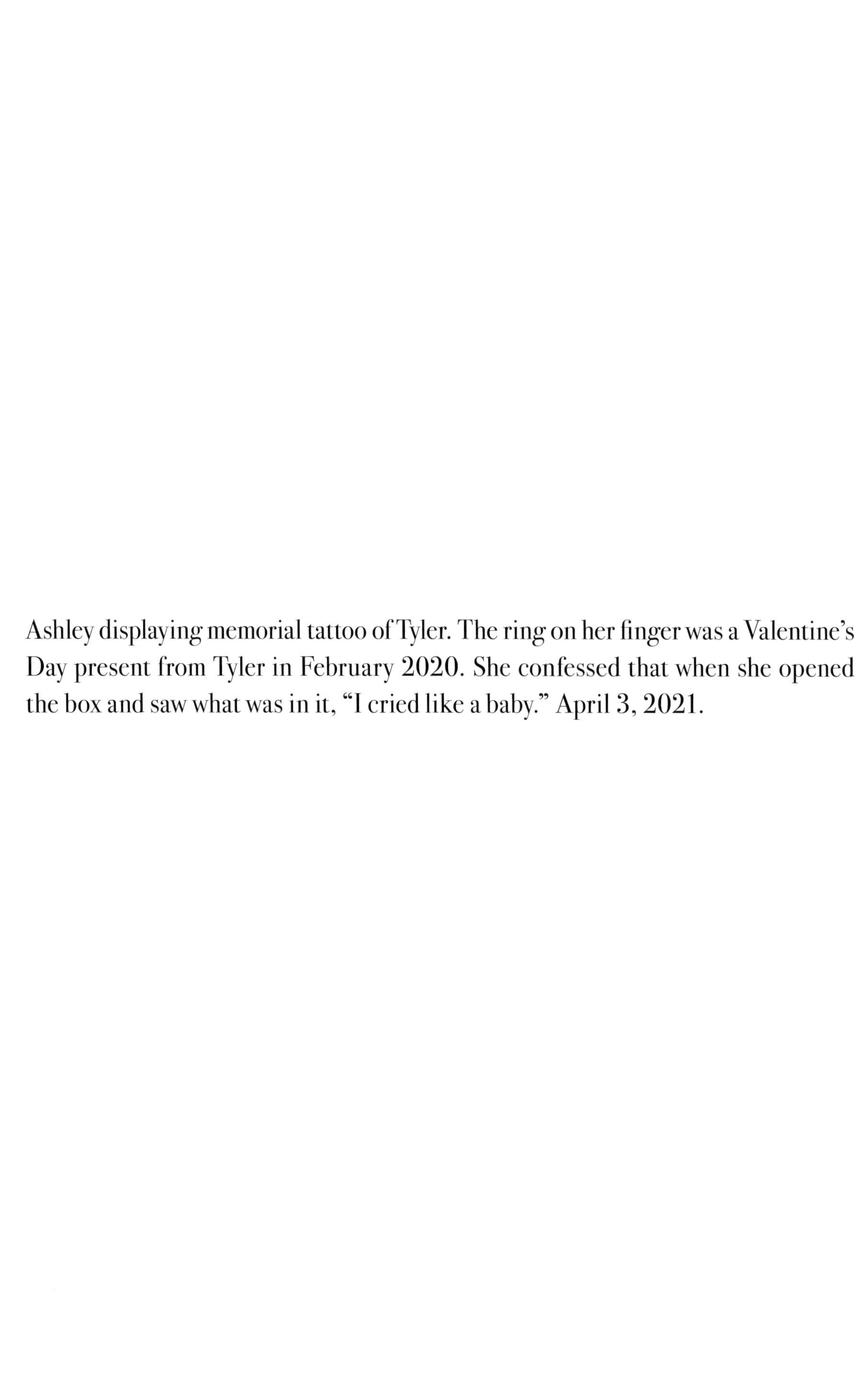

Ashley displaying memorial tattoo of Tyler. The ring on her finger was a Valentine's Day present from Tyler in February 2020. She confessed that when she opened the box and saw what was in it, "I cried like a baby." April 3, 2021.

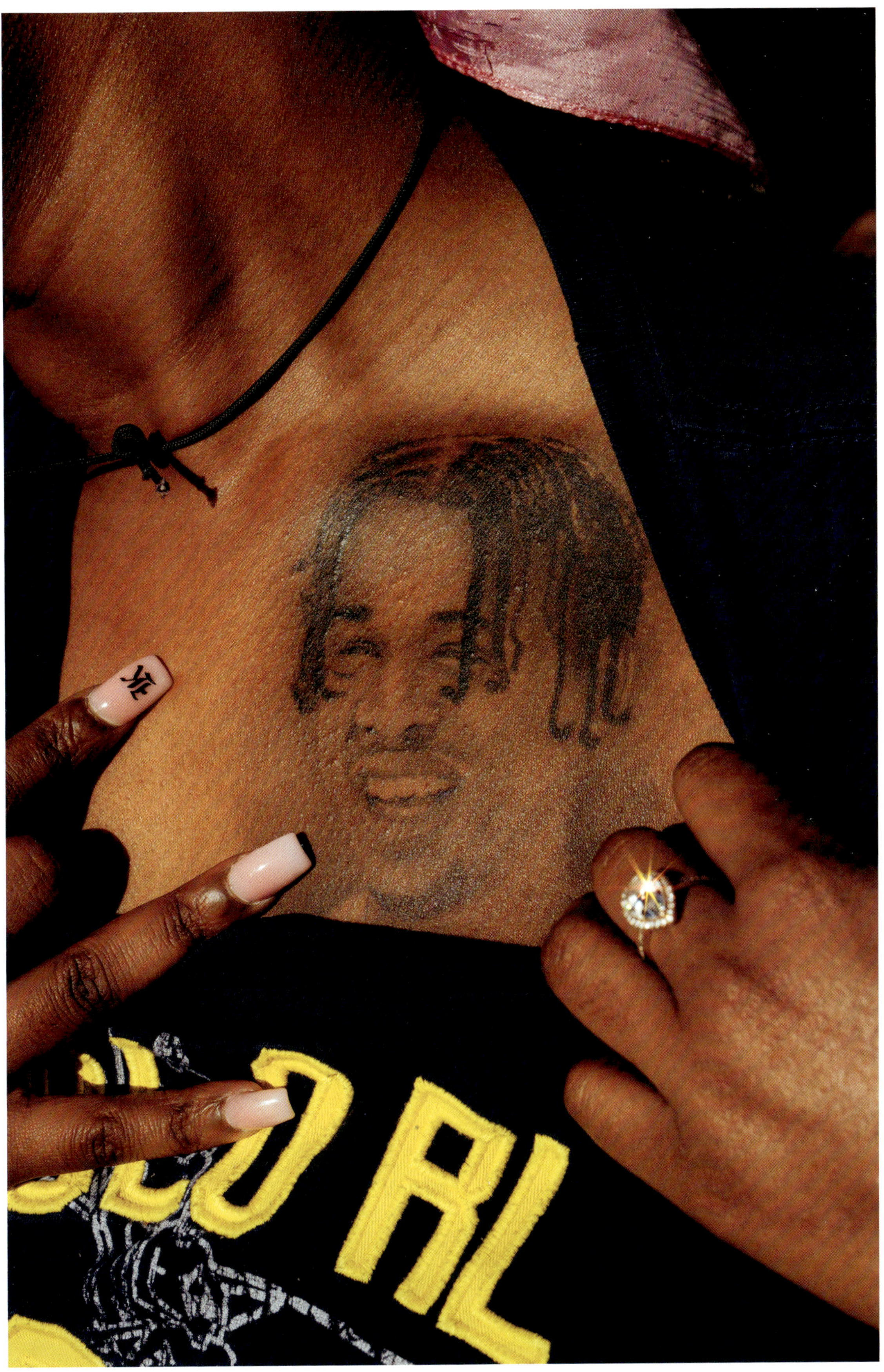

Tyler with Kobe Bryant in Santa Barbara, California; summer 2012.

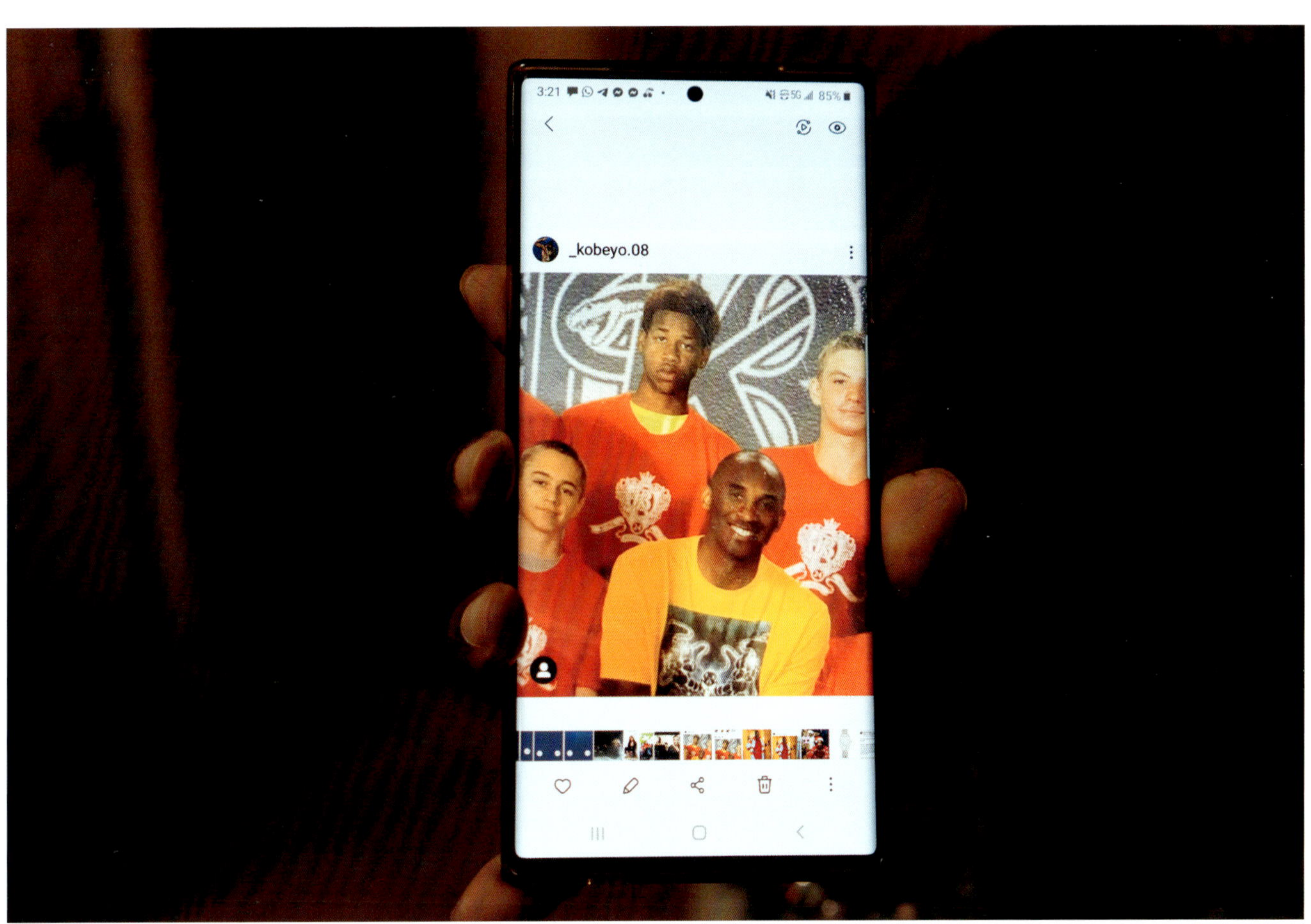
3:21
85%
_kobeyo.08

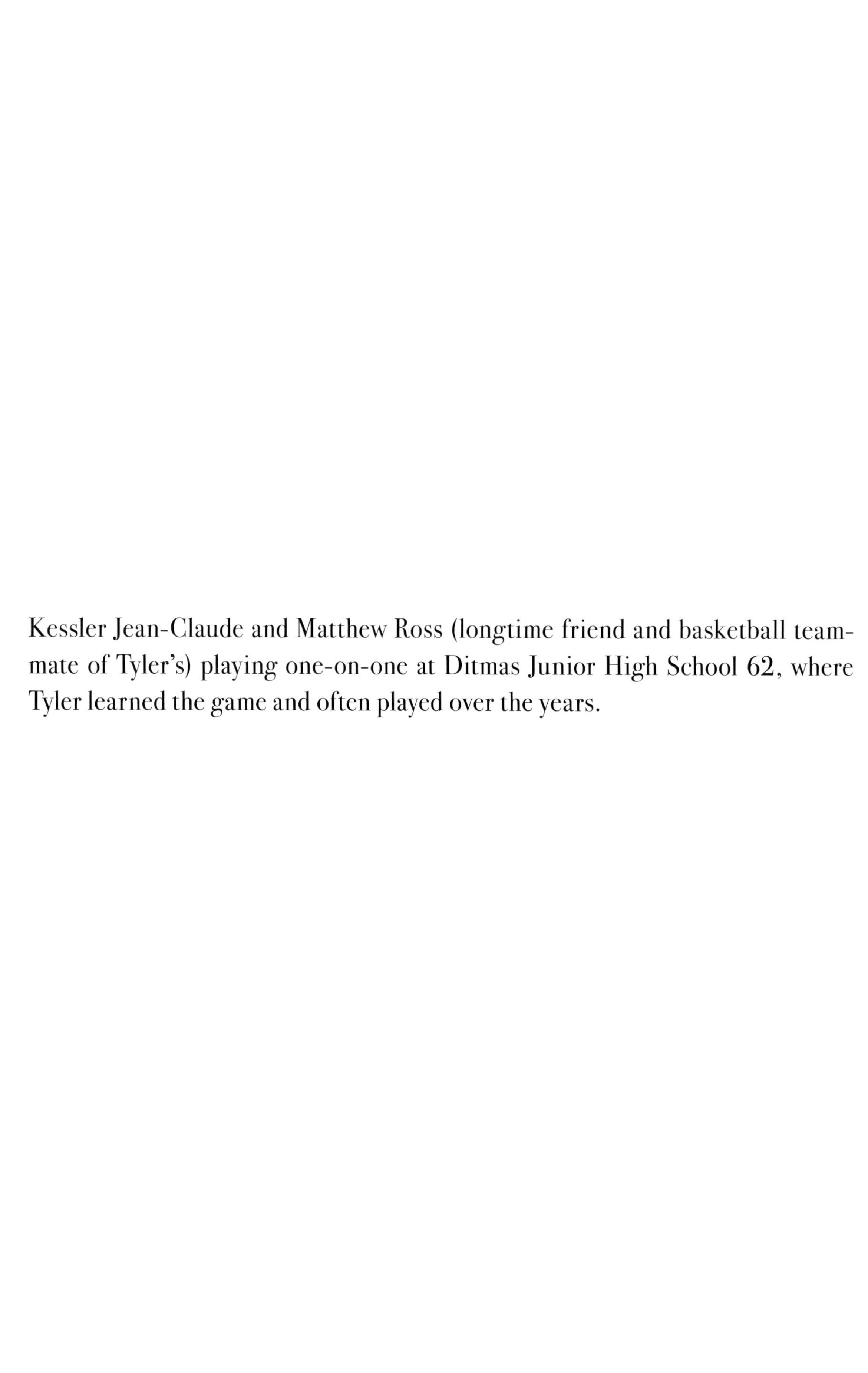

Kessler Jean-Claude and Matthew Ross (longtime friend and basketball teammate of Tyler's) playing one-on-one at Ditmas Junior High School 62, where Tyler learned the game and often played over the years.

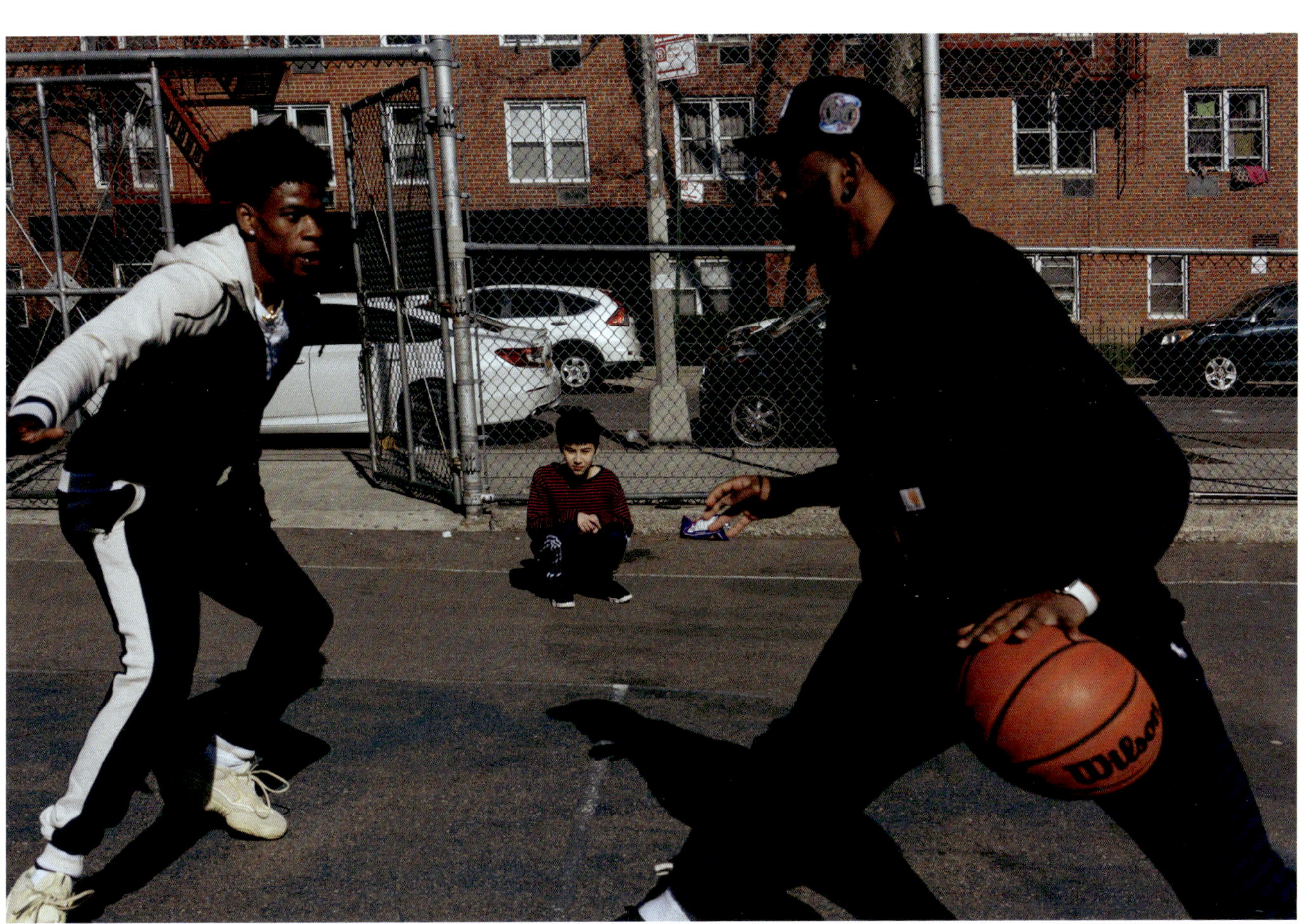
Wilson

Ditmas Junior High School 62 playground; April 3, 2021.

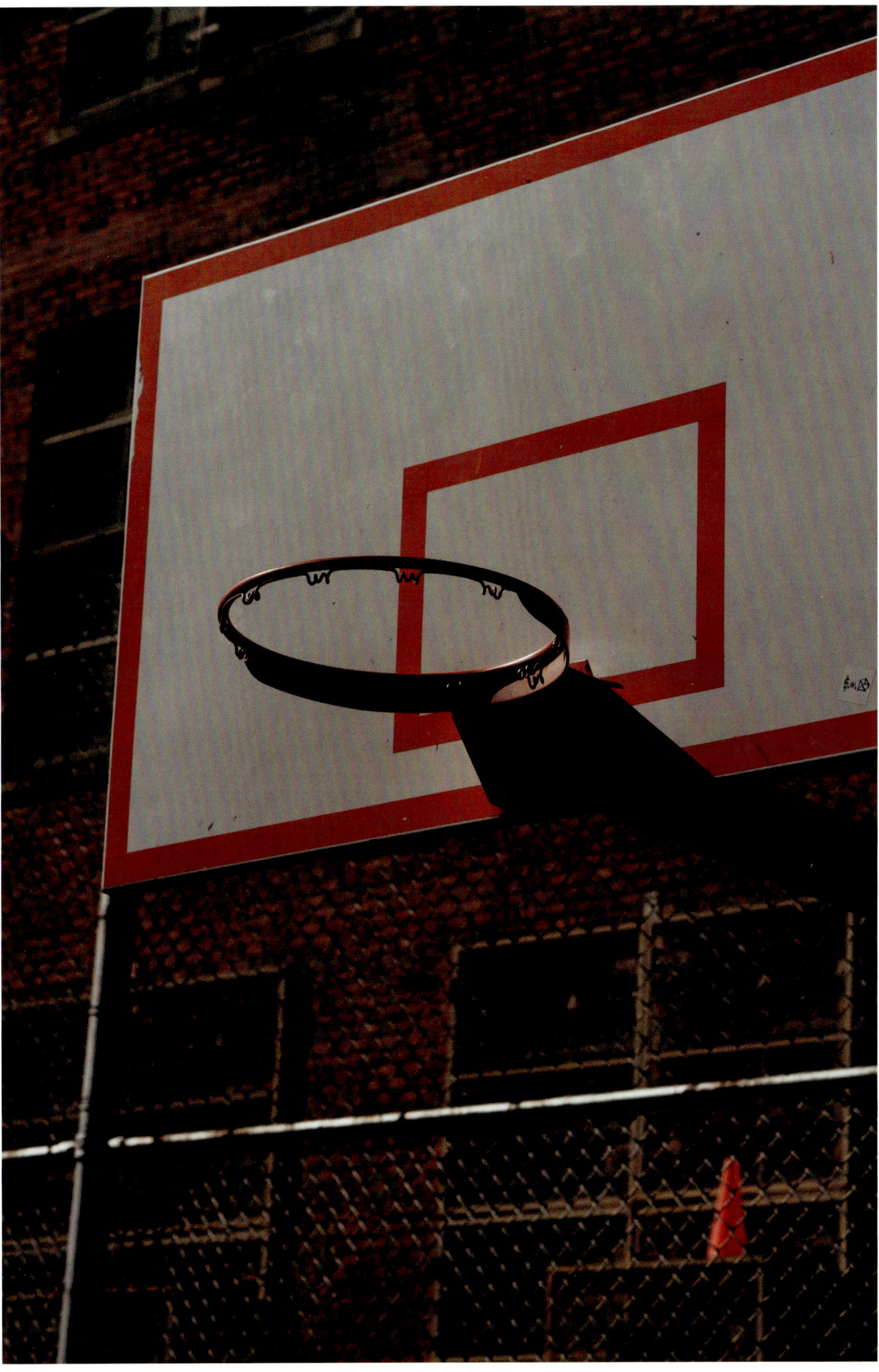

Matthew Ross; April 3, 2021.

He was at the house on the night of the murder. When Shayne called to announce that Tyler had collapsed on the sidewalk, Matthew was one of many family members and friends who ran out into the street to look for the corner where Tyler was stretched out on the pavement. He was the first person to arrive, and when Tyler saw him, he reached out and took hold of Matthew's hand. Kareem and Shomari soon followed, and from that moment until the ambulance pulled up at the corner some minutes later, Kareem was on his knees, frantically applying pressure to his cousin's wounds and doing everything in his power to keep Tyler conscious.

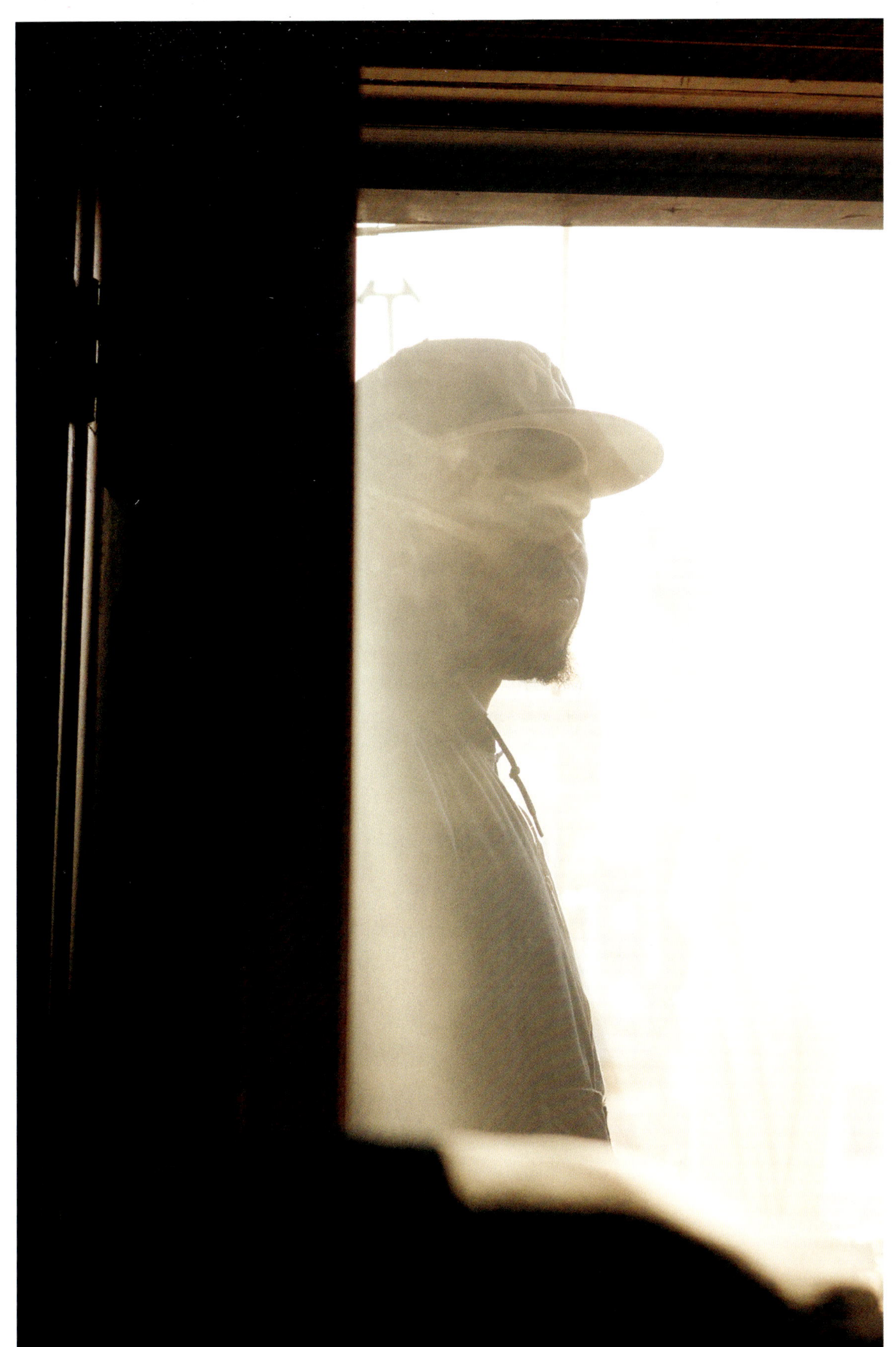

Joshua Robles, longtime friend and member of the inner circle; April 23, 2021.

"Talking about it now, my stomach is turning *(starts to shake)*. I wouldn't know how to put it into words, but it's a feeling I wouldn't wish on anybody."

"All of us are dealing with it differently. Everybody has their own different feelings. Shayne and Shomari–we won't ever know how they feel–and Shayne and Shomari will never know how Mommy feels."

When asked how he was dealing with it, he answered: "I'm trying to accept it, that he's gone, but he's not really gone. He's here, but I can't see him...I'd rather cry by myself than cry in front of them [his friends], because it's like a domino effect, and if one person cries, another person will think about it and cry. I don't know. I just know he wouldn't want us crying. If no one there ever had a reason to live, they have a reason to live now. *(Clicking lighter nervously)*. He was younger, but he always felt like my older brother."

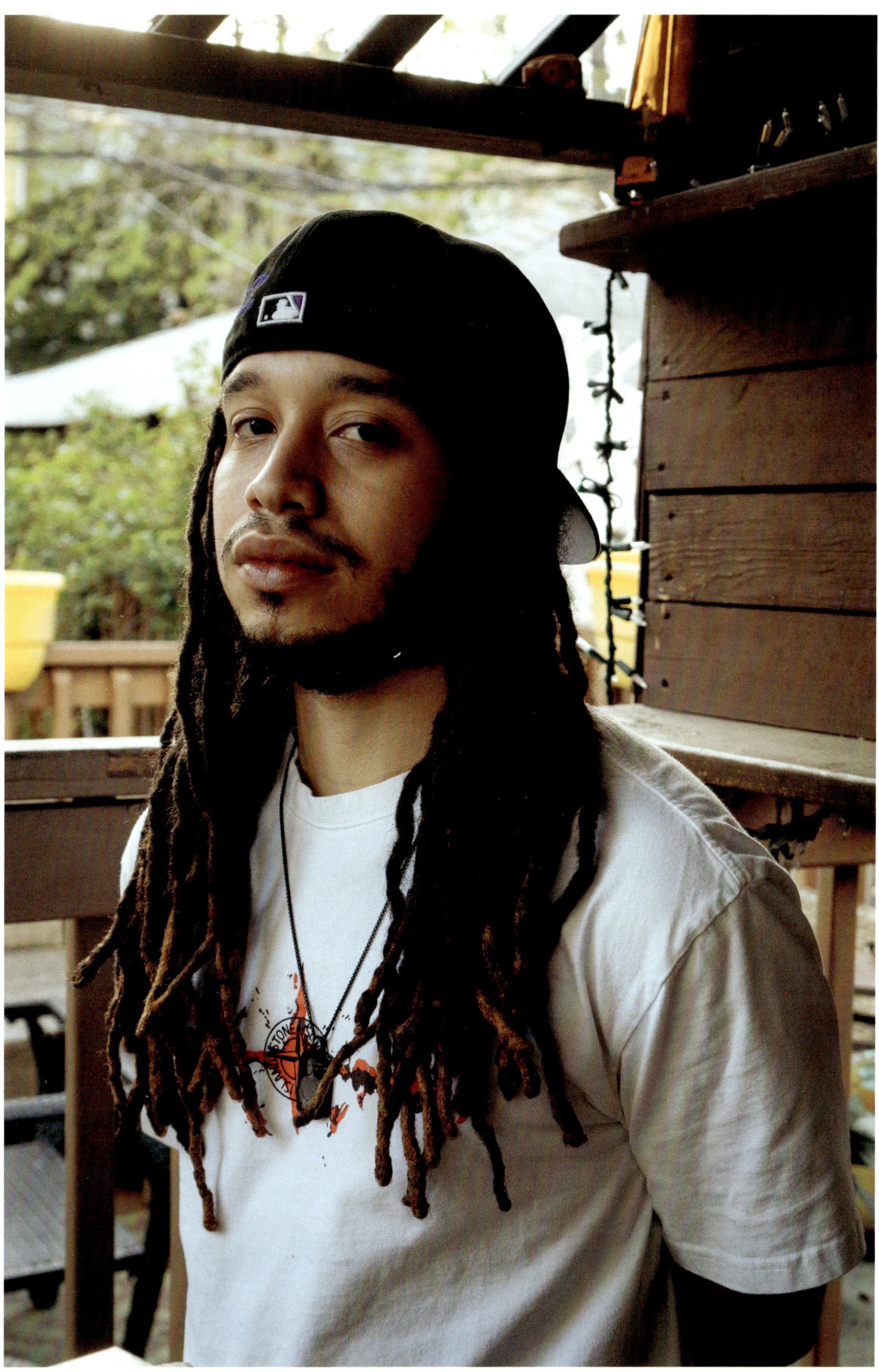

Hershon Teslaint, events photographer and another close friend of Tyler's since middle school; April 3, 2021.

After an abrupt move from Orlando to Brooklyn when he was in the sixth grade, the young Hershon felt disoriented and displaced—"an outcast," as he put it—and if not for the equally young Tyler, who reached out and befriended him, the transition to Brooklyn life would have been immensely more difficult. "Tyler was the first person who never judged me," he said, and now that Tyler is gone, he goes on struggling to make sense of what happened. "Since he left us, I don't know who to talk to anymore."

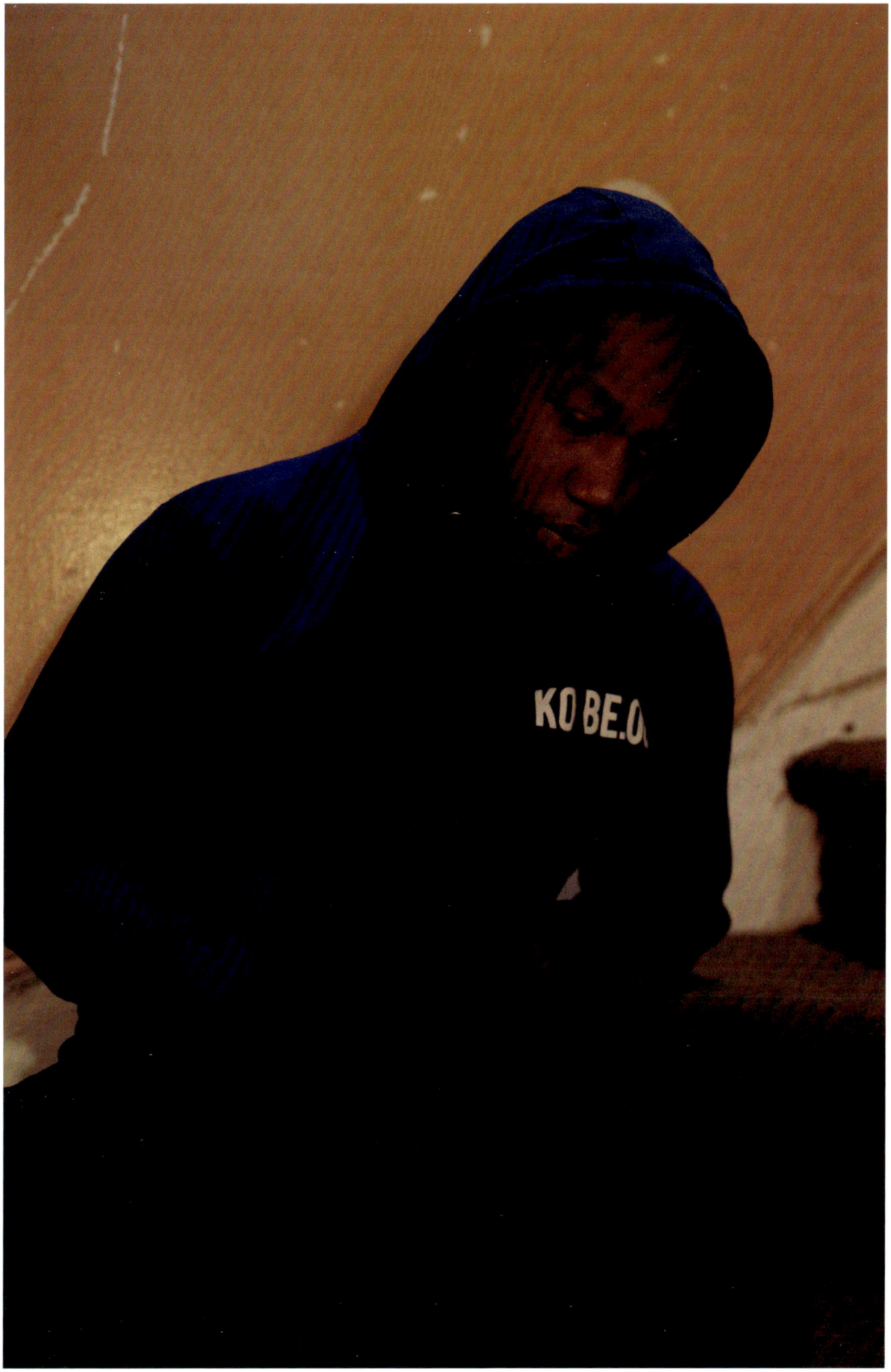

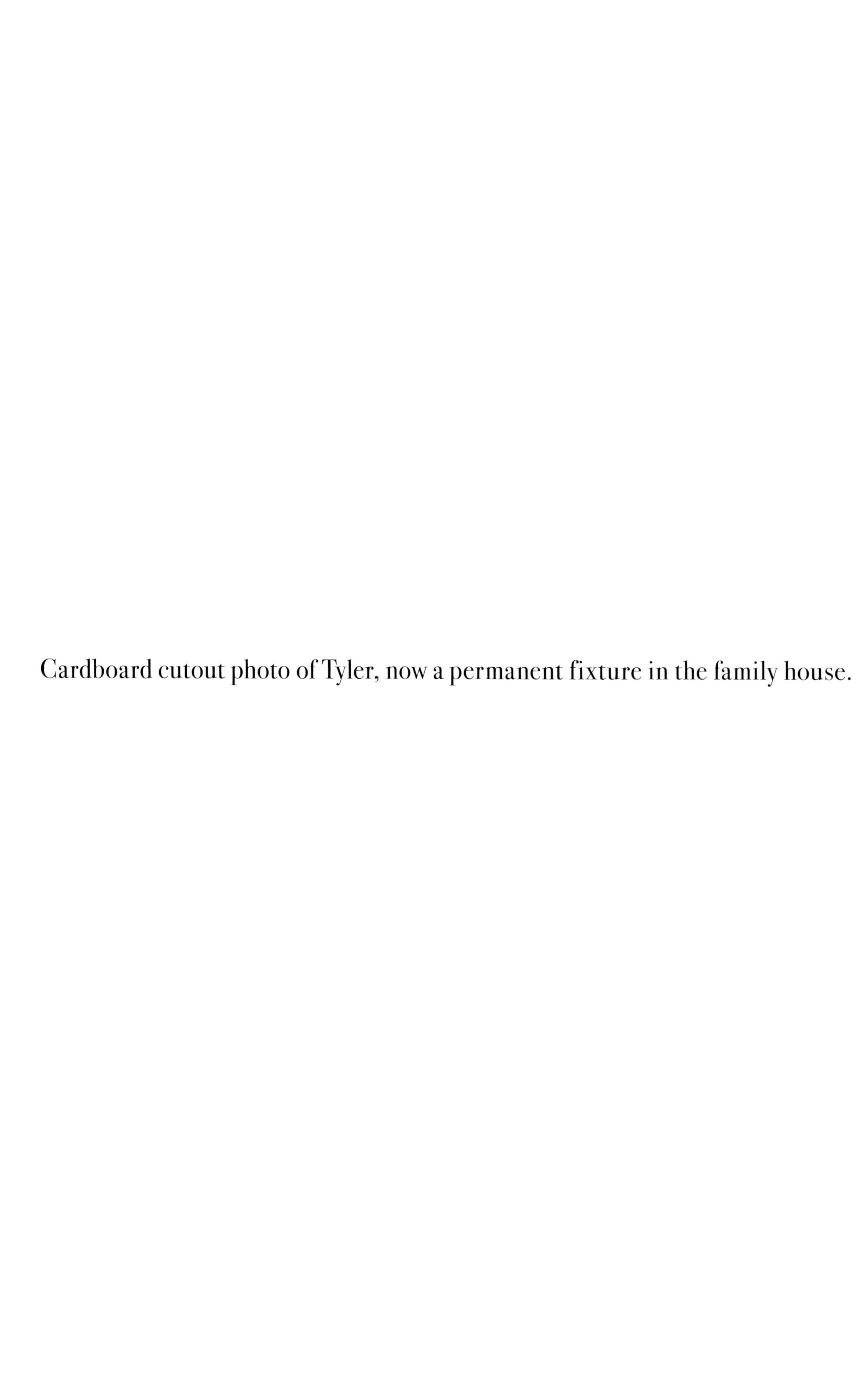

Cardboard cutout photo of Tyler, now a permanent fixture in the family house.

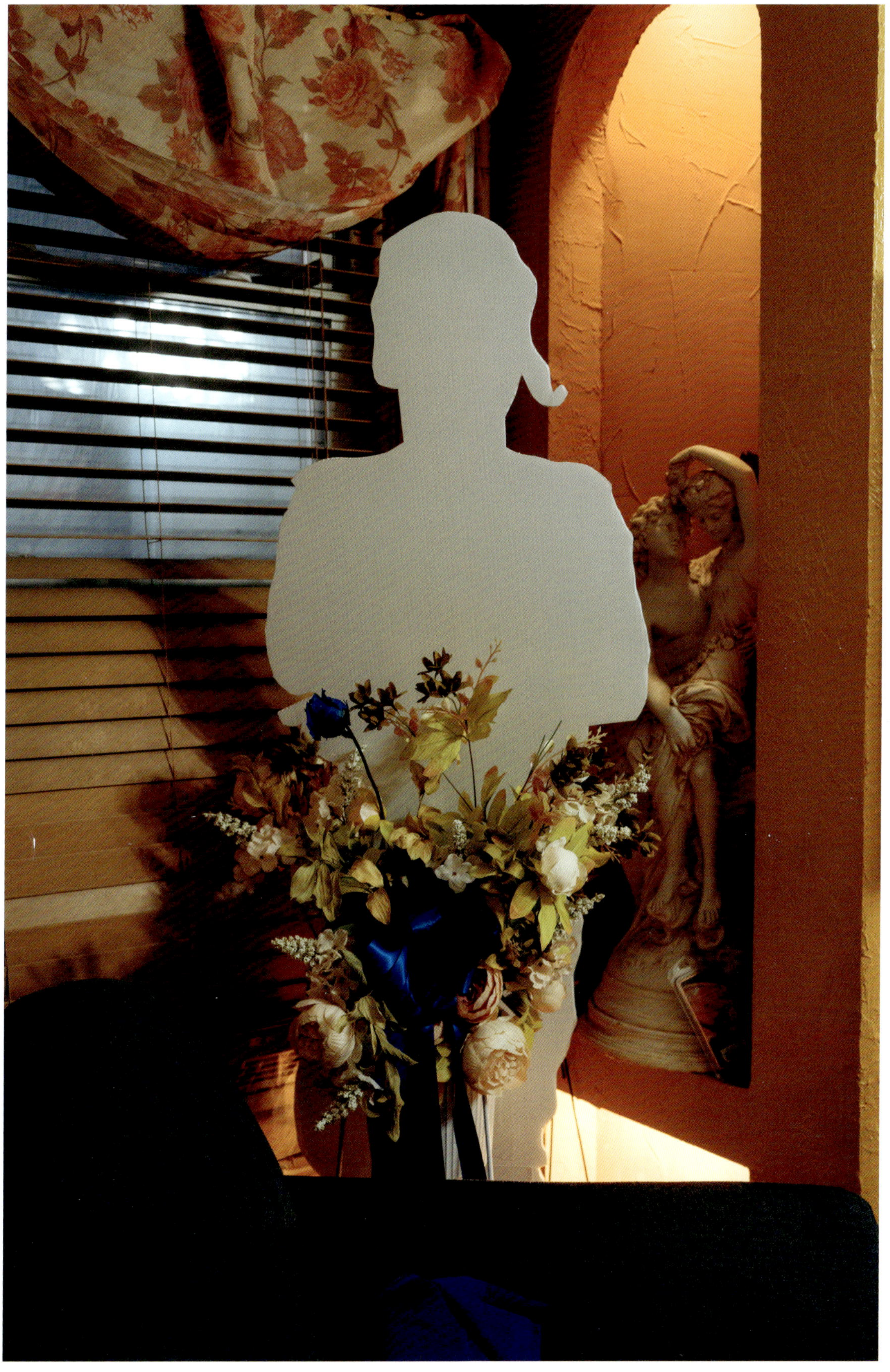

Canarsie Cemetery, Brooklyn. The cemetery is in the process of being expanded to the west, but work has been slowed by restrictions during the Covid-19 pandemic. Tyler's plot is located in this new, unfinished area, which has been opened prematurely to accommodate the increase of deaths caused by the virus.

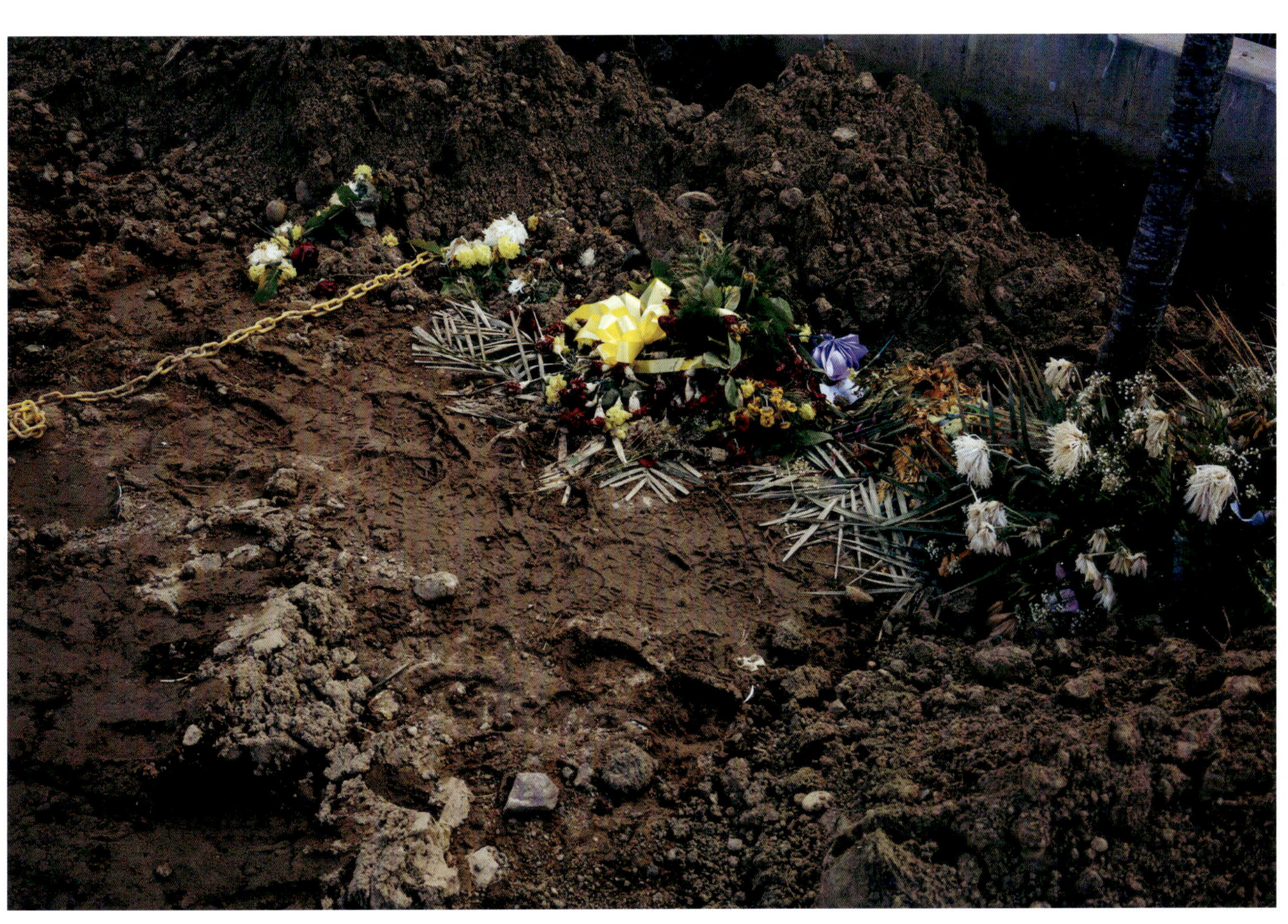

Kareem Eusebe searching for his cousin’s grave site; March 6, 2021.

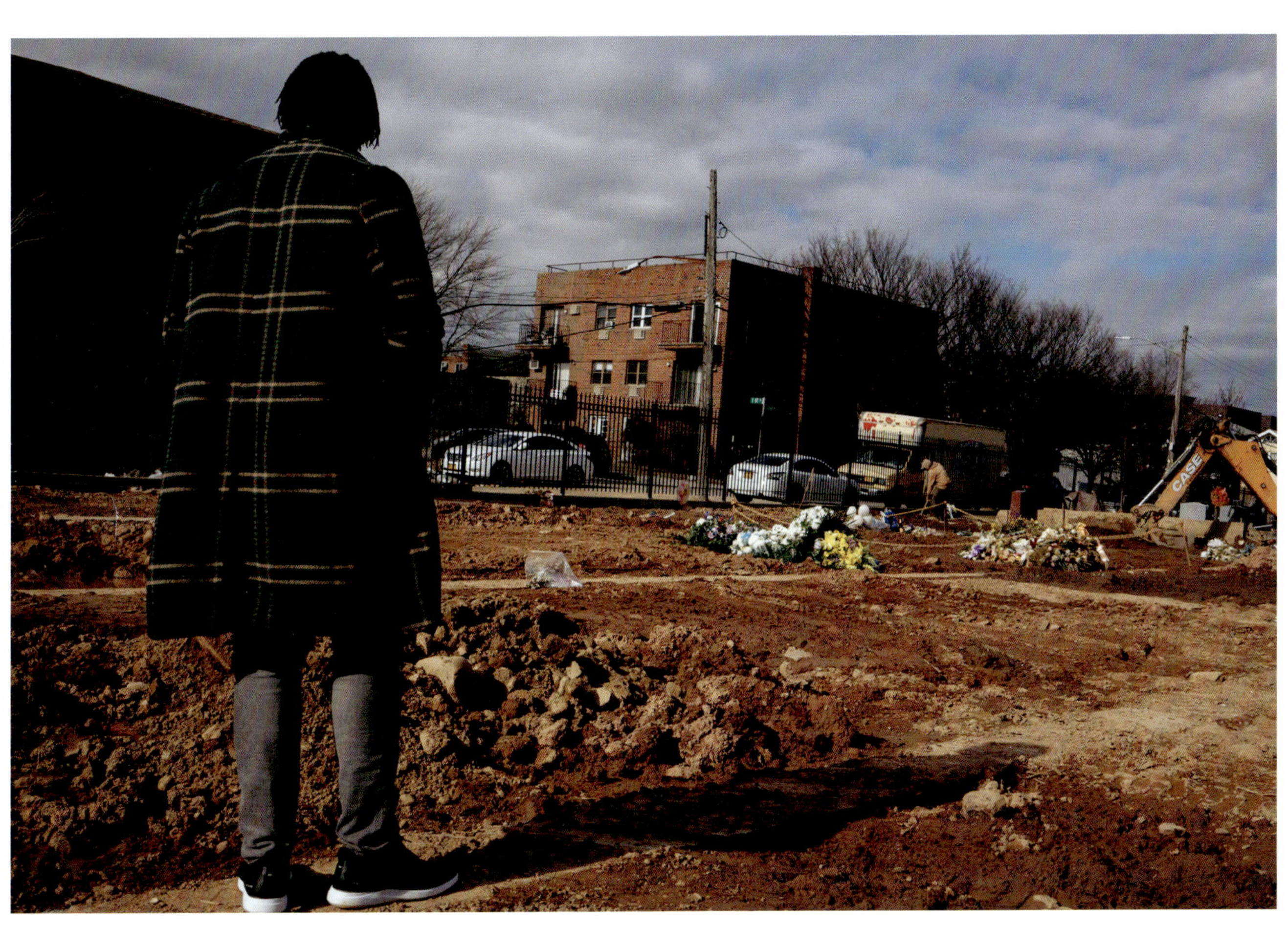
CASE

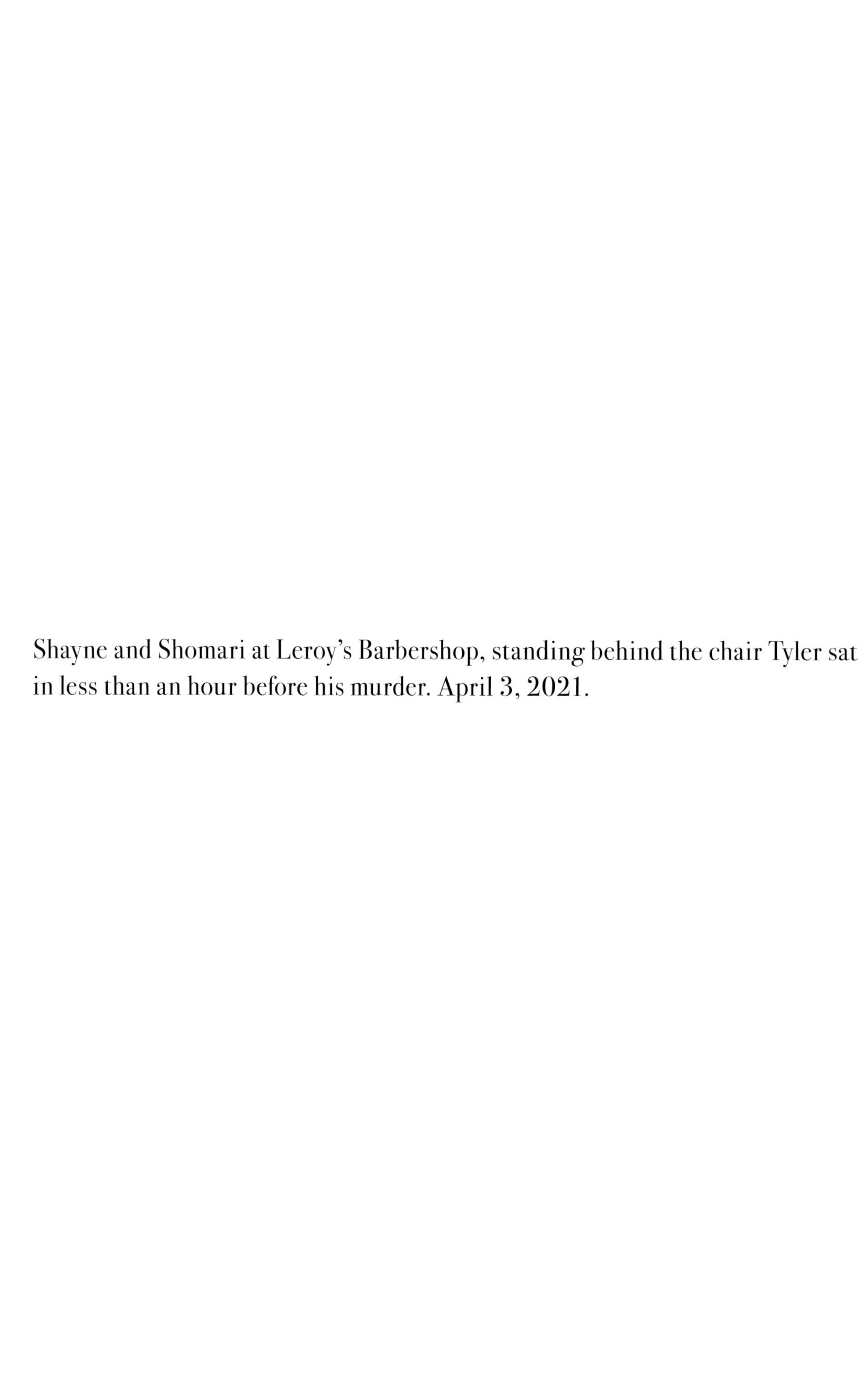

Shayne and Shomari at Leroy's Barbershop, standing behind the chair Tyler sat in less than an hour before his murder. April 3, 2021.

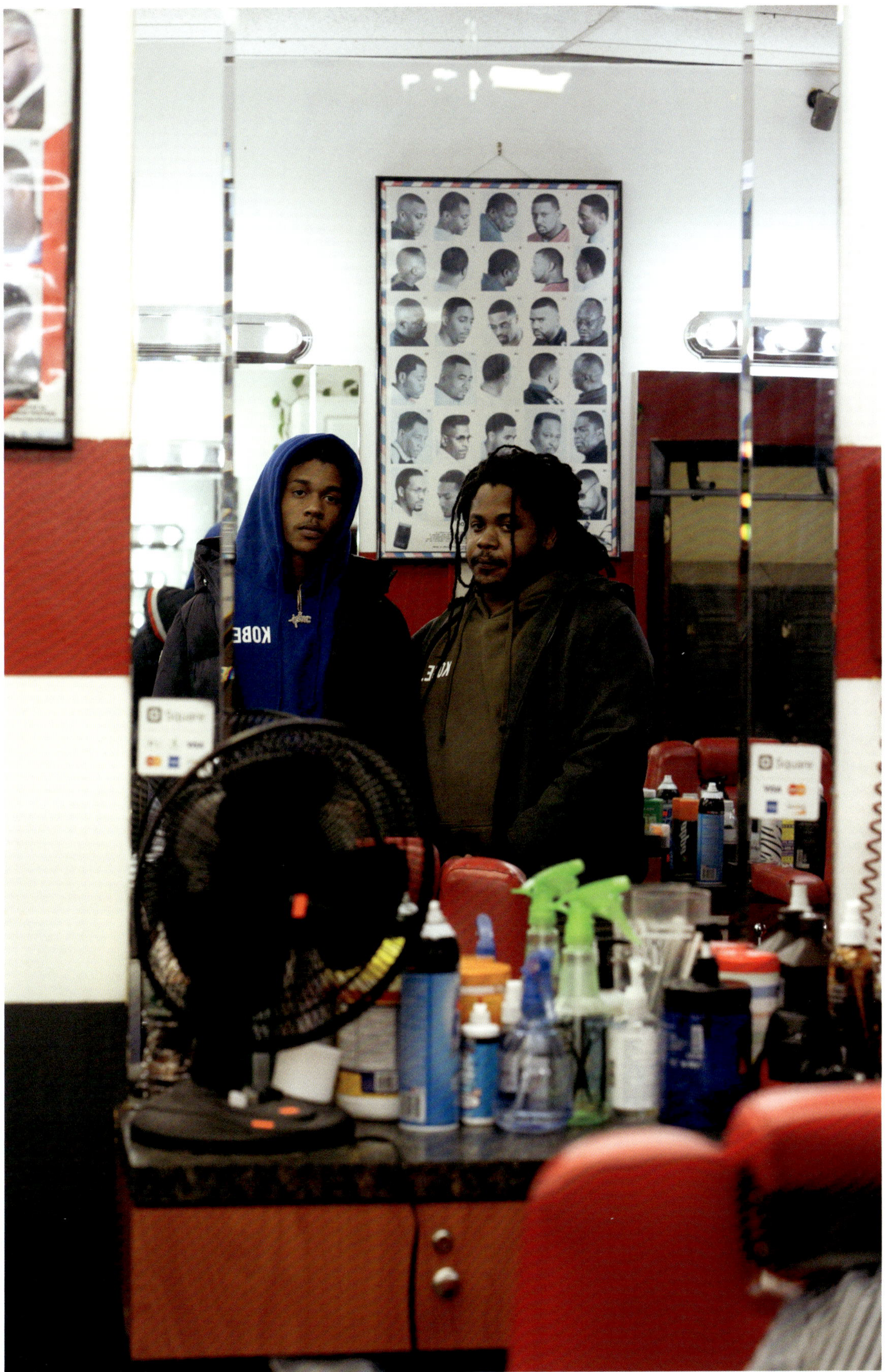

Sherma and Shayne at the candle ceremony in front of the house on the evening of April 23, 2021, the four-month anniversary of Tyler's death.

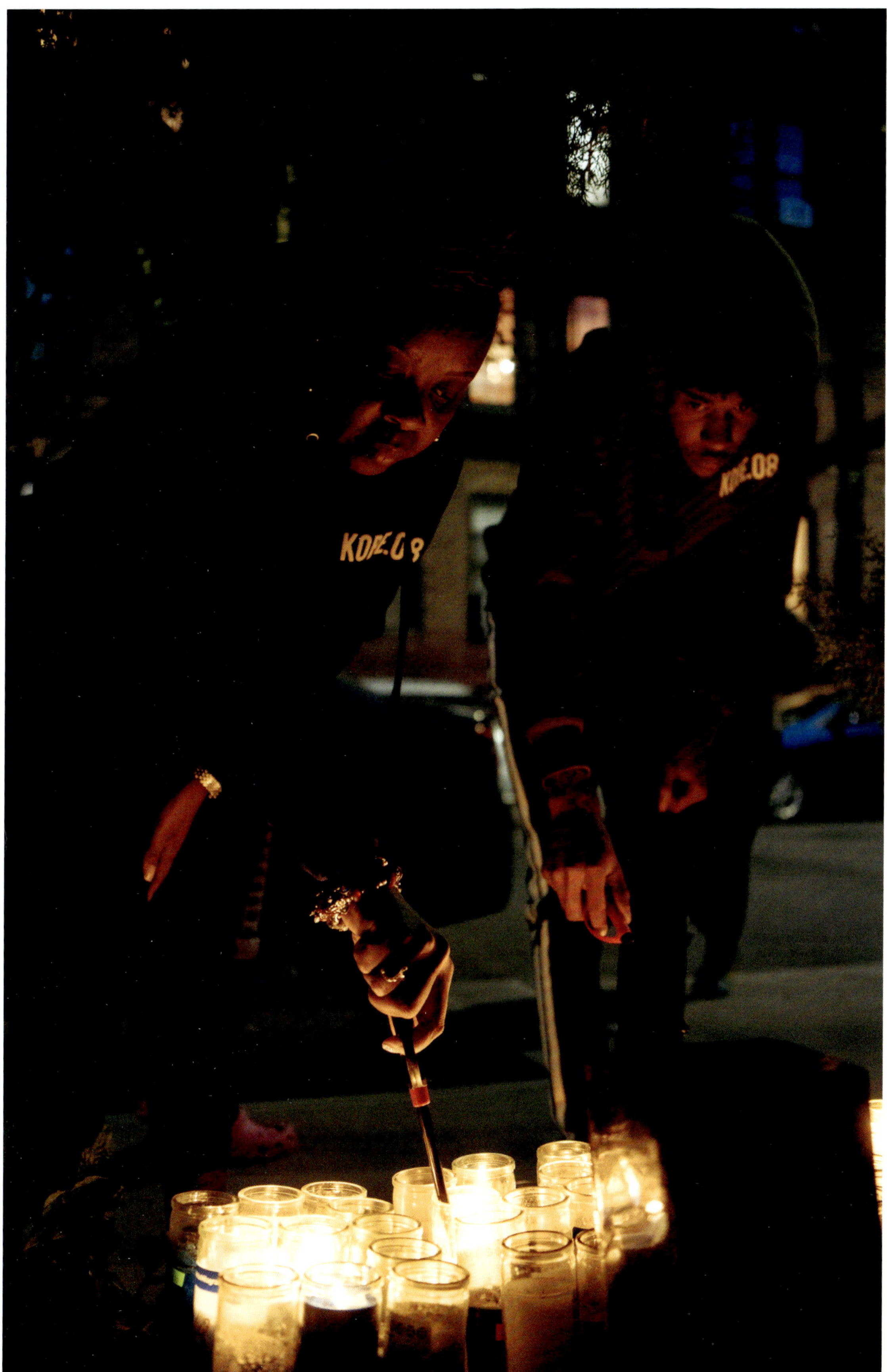

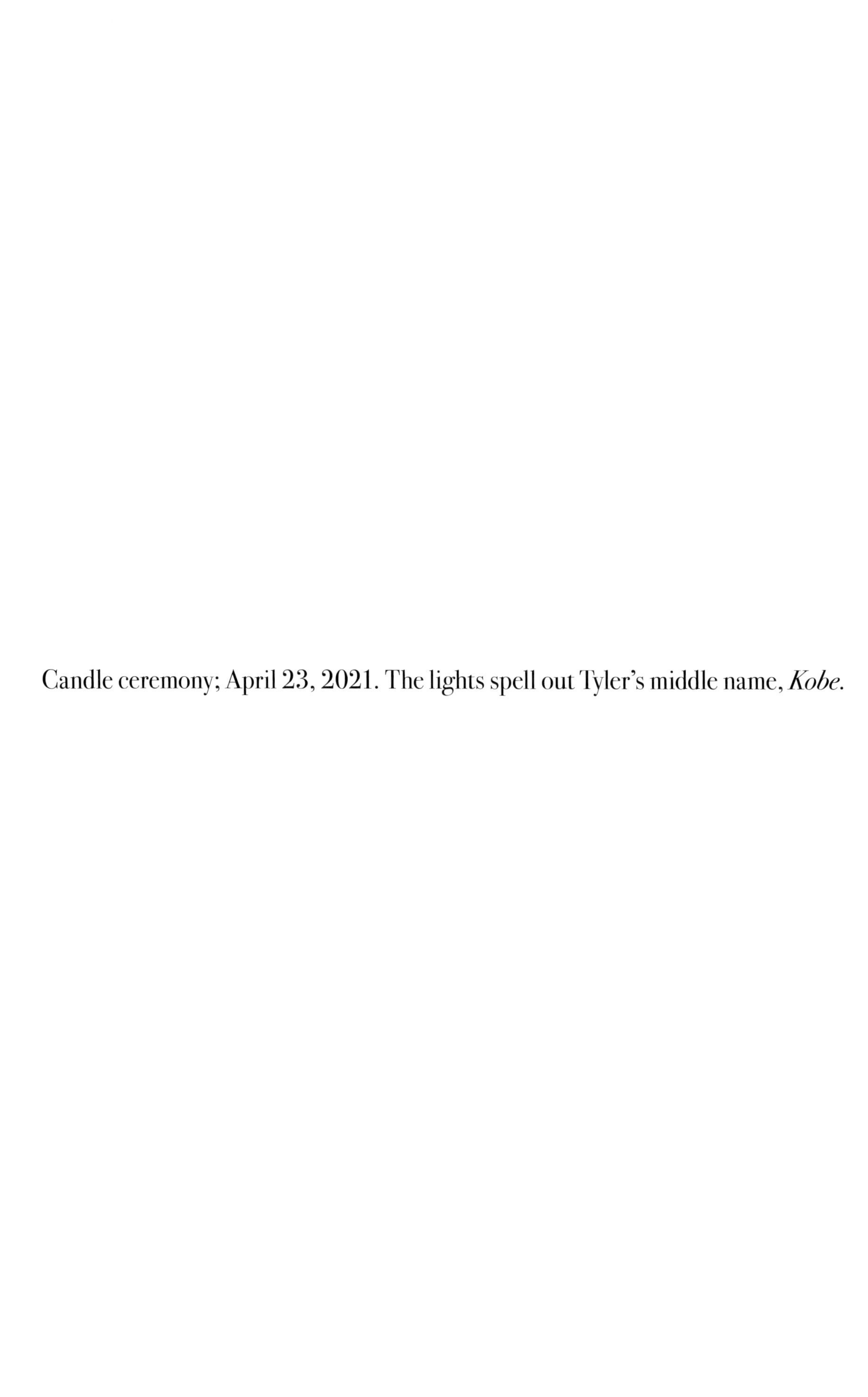

Candle ceremony; April 23, 2021. The lights spell out Tyler's middle name, *Kobe*.

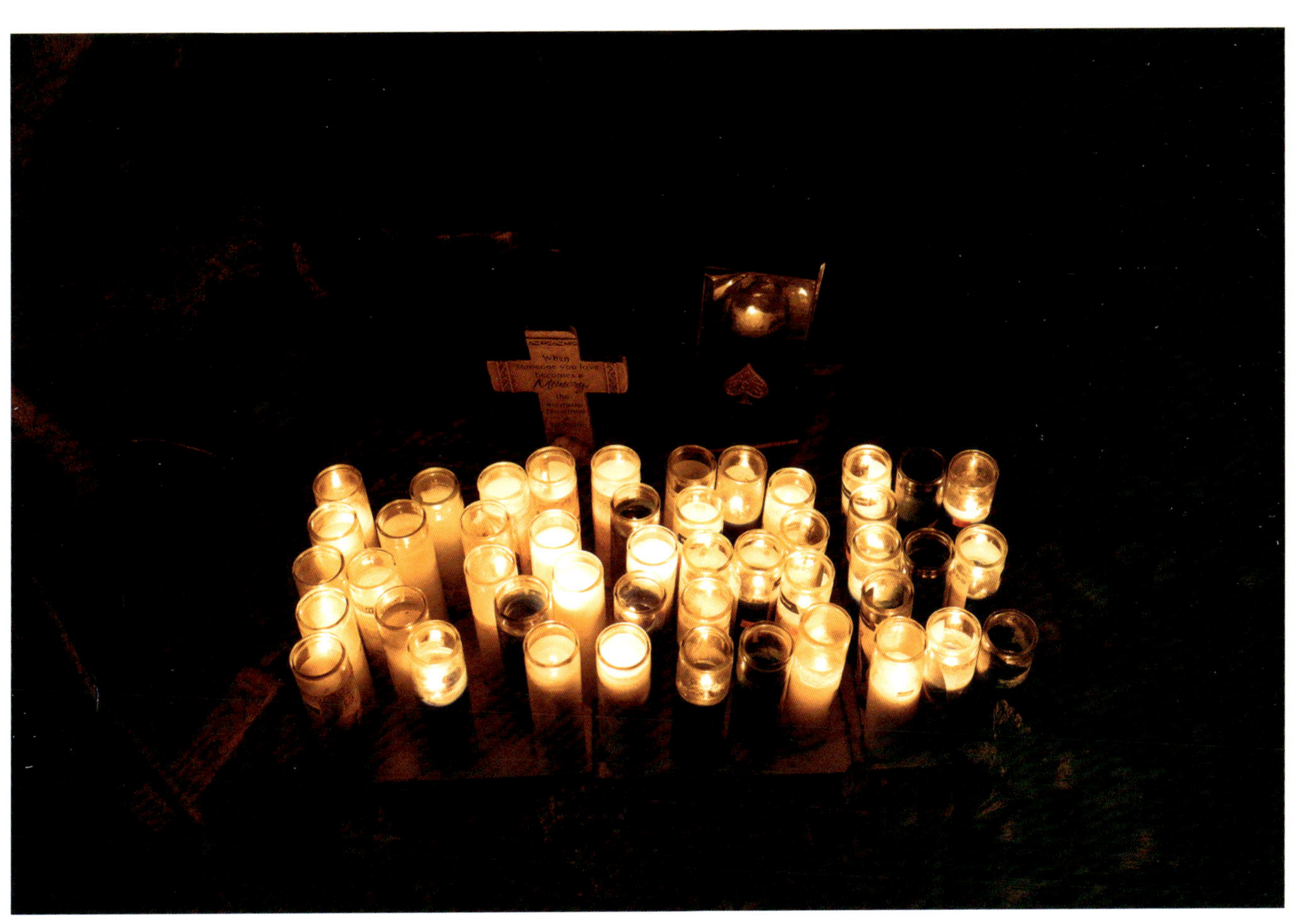
When
someone you love
becomes a
Memory,
the

My deepest gratitude to Shayne Nichols, Shomari Nichols, Garnet Nichols, Garnet Nichols, Jr., Ashley Duverneau, Brittany Augustine, Kareem Eusebe, Vera Nichols, Brianna Augustine, Desirée Chambers, Carlene Chambers, Elizabeth Chambers, Kessler Jean-Claude, Matthew Ross, Joshua Robles, and Herson Teslaint for participating in this project. I would especially like to thank Sherma Chambers, for without her this book would not exist.

I would also like to thank Sophie Auster, Paul Auster, Siri Hustvedt, Michael Zilkha, Chris Heiser, Kelsey Nolan, Rachel Eliza Griffiths, Bonnie Briant, Christopher Anderson, Peter van Agtmael, Adam Ferguson, and Ted King for their support.

-Spencer Ostrander

PUBLISHED BY
ZE Books of Houston, TX
(in partnership with Unnamed Press of Los Angeles, CA)
3262 Westheimer Road, #467 Houston, TX 77098
www.zebooks.com

COPYRIGHT
Text Copyright © 2022 by Paul Auster
Image Copyright © 2022 by Spencer Ostrander
Foreword © 2022 by Sherma Chambers

BOOK DESIGN & TYPESETTING
Bonnie Briant Design

NOTICE
Long Live King Kobe is a work of nonfiction.
From its inception, it was a collaborative project between photographer, author, and its subjects.
The Chambers-Nichols family and all persons featured in the book have approved
the book (and all images included herein) for publication.

ISBN
9781736309322

Library of Congress control number available upon request.
Manufactured in Canada

First ZE Books Printing: May 2022
2 4 6 8 9 7 5 3 1
First Edition

DISCARD